DEM☉S

Demos is an independent think tank committed to radical thinking on the long-term problems facing the UK and other advanced industrial societies.

It aims to develop ideas – both theoretical and practical – to help shape the politics of the twenty-first century, and to improve the breadth and quality of political debate.

Demos publishes books and a regular journal and undertakes substantial empirical and policy oriented research projects. Demos is a registered charity.

In all its work Demos brings together people from a wide range of backgrounds in business, academia, government, the voluntary sector and the media to share and cross-fertilise ideas and experiences.

For further information and
subscription details please contact:
Demos
The Mezzanine
Elizabeth House
39 York Road
London
SE1 7NQ
email: mail@demos.co.uk
www.demos.co.uk

The Protest Ethic
*How the anti-globalisation movement
challenges social democracy*

John Lloyd

DEM⊙S

First published in 2001 by
Demos
The Mezzanine
Elizabeth House
39 York Road
London SE1 7NQ

ISBN 1 84180 009 0
Typeset by Discript
Cover design by The Set Up

Contents

Acknowledgements

Thanks for guidance to Anthony Barnett, Anthony Giddens, David Goodhart, Ian Hargreaves, David Held, Mary Kaldor, David Lea, Charles Leadbeater, Philippe Legrain, Vladimir Mau, Frederic Michel, Ziauddin Sardar and Martin Wolf.

Thanks to Tom Bentley, Eddie Gibb and all at Demos.

John Lloyd
October 2001

1. Introduction: The political responses to globalisation

The political responses to globalisation – however that is defined – are still being shaped. The phenomenon is new, contested and heavily politicised: it cuts across old ideological boundaries, which were anyway melting and changing. But it is possible to detect some fuzzy outlines.

The pure market response to globalisation is to insist on the openness of economies to trade, investment and international, as well as internal, competition. Rules that are agreed between states are important here, as are the institutions – such as the World Trade Organisation – that seek to make these rules uniform and universal in application. The rich countries of the world and those nations that strive to be among their number adhere, at least formally, to the rules. The key actors in this system remain states, and the agreements reached between them.

Many states cannot or do not wish to adhere to these rules. They may be too poor and/or badly governed to participate at any more than a minimal level in the world economy. Their governing elites may have cultural or religious reasons for not wanting uncontrolled modernisation – seeing, correctly, that openness to the world economy carries with it the importation of Western culture. In some cases, these states' elites are actively hostile to many features of globalisation, seeing it as dominated by the US, secular and materialistic. They believe it should be shunned, as far as is practicable; and if its products are consumed, then its ideology should certainly be rejected.

Between a pure market response and a pure refusal to enter the global economy – compare the Cayman Islands and North Korea – a range of accommodations is evident. Each state has its own particular way of relating to the global economy, and that can be altered substantially (as in the US) through a change of government: one of many instances contradicting the view that 'globalisation renders governments powerless'.

In broad terms, however, the wealthy Western states base their economies and growth on open markets and relatively free trade, and have democratic polities. They have preached the rhetoric of openness and secured a phase of prosperity by combining partial openness with equal trading partners and increasing economic and social opportunities for citizens who are not socially excluded. Key domains, such as trade and immigration, are protected from less developed parts of the world.

The more advanced among the developing countries oscillate between emulation of the prescribed liberal economic policies and protectionism coupled with state subsidies. Their politics can be unstable, tending to be at least formally democratic, but sometimes retaining authoritarian government. In China, for example, the rapid liberalisation of trade and much of the domestic economy has been so successful that the country is likely to enter the World Trade Organisation; but that economic liberalisation is coupled with a very large, heavily subsidised state sector, while politics remain a Communist Party monopoly.

The Western left has produced two main responses to globalisation. The most vivid and widely known is that of the global movements.[1] They have established themselves as uncompromising, even apocalyptic, critics of capitalist globalisation. They are diverse, but tend to agree that the effects of globalisation, defined as 'capitalist globalisation', are harmful – to the poor, to the environment and to animals. The only people who gain from globalisation are, they believe, the rich, overwhelmingly concentrated in the West.

The global movements have been painting on a global economic and political canvas, in ways the social democratic left has not. They have highlighted the misery and drudgery, oppression, hopelessness and voicelessness of much of the world's population. They also impart, especially to young people, a sense of dedication to the cause of others less fortunate than most in the Western world. The global movements prompt the left to confront its responsibility to do global politics.

The centre-left has found itself at something of a loss in the face of these new movements. Social democrats have claimed the rights and responsibilities of power, and must appeal and deliver to mass electorates. Thus governments of the left, which at the end of the 1990s were in power in almost all of the richest states in the world, became the targets of movements that protested allegiance to many of the goals to which the democratic left parties were historically committed, and which they still believe they serve.

The difficulties faced by the centre-left are in part those of a democratic movement confronting an activist one. Social democracy eschews the violence promoted by a minority among these movements. It distances itself not just from the attempts to destroy property and attack the police (which many of the movements themselves condemned), but also from the demonstrators' clear intent to stop or intimidate the meetings around which they clustered. These were, after all, meetings at which centre-left governments were often in the majority, and at which projects to further combat poverty and assist development were on the agenda.

Social democrats could not descend to the fevered anti-Americanism that marks the rhetoric of many of the groups. Until the election of George W Bush at the end of 2000, the European centre left and the US Democratic parties had come together in discussions on policy and ideas as never before, discussions that addressed the nature of globalisation and the centre-left's response to it. After 11 September, centre-left governments were united, at least in words, behind the US. Some of the global movements, aided by elements of the far left, took a position which, stripped of its equivocation, held that the US had 'asked for it'.

Social democracy cannot take the position of many of the groups: explicit or implicit anti-capitalism. It requires a healthy capitalist system to achieve its reformist goals. Capitalism is currently the only grand economic system available; the issue for social democrats now, as it was (if less clearly) in the 20th century, is how to mould and shape it through the political process to meet popular – and global – needs.

Left governments cannot expect to win favour or maintain coherence by making ad hoc concessions to the global movements' demands. These can make matters worse for developing countries: the voice of the global movements is not their voice, and the movements' aims cannot comprehend the trade-offs that developing countries must make in order to advance. What is at stake here is not a global equivalent of a bargain between social partners on wages, where a compromise between a high and a low figure brings agreement. It is a matter of different, sometimes fundamentally different, approaches to global development. Above all, it is the difference between activism infused with ideals and democratic politics infused with ideals.

Yet the left governments are constrained to admit that the global movements have found new ways of using political power which they themselves sought to exercise. The movements can generate widespread public sympathy and a degree of mobilisation from diverse social and ideological groupings. They are able to use networks freely and inventively, and to inspire action through information and ideas on the internet. They are able to generate interest on, sometimes to dominate, the network media in a way that makes conventional political communication look stale and tired.

They are able to do so because they do not have the capacity or responsibility for ordering priorities, reconciling competing interests among their constituencies, maintaining public accountability or implementing practical solutions, which are essential characteristics of politics and governance. They cannot be an alternative to democratic government, in spite of claims to the contrary. Yet their challenges demand a response from social democrats currently occupying the structures of formal political power, especially because political parties, in decline almost everywhere in the advanced world, are struggling to adapt to the more fluid and network-based environments in which the new movements thrive.

They have also given sketches of answers to the questions that have become more urgent since 11 September – the questions begged by the coming together of global issues to form a constant constituency of concern: a series of inequalities and injustices about which the left cannot feel indifferent. These sketches usually exist at the level of idealism, with little sense of real politics, and make no effort to begin the compromises and bargaining that the realisation of ideals demands. But ideals were the foundation of social democracy, and must remain its inspiration.

The argument here is that, in creating a global market, we are creating willy-nilly the outlines of a global society. The left must bring to the table the concerns that inform its domestic practice – greater equality, social justice, the right of free expression, non-exploitative relations, personal (including economic) security. A central element of the history of the centre-left is an effort to bring to politics a systemic view of the world, providing a context within which the activities of the market can be both shaped and evaluated. This aspiration has partly been lost in the effort to win national power. But without an account of the market's workings globally, and its effect on the majority of the population who are poor, there can be no sustained effort to diminish poverty. Giving that account practical application in a new era of globalisation is the next task of the left.

One sketch of a social democratic global approach was given in Tony Blair's speech to the Labour Party conference in October 2001. It proposed a greatly increased aid effort, the assumption of much more responsibility for the alleviation of misery and oppression, and a much more active and more readily triggered ability to intervene militarily to protect victims in combat zones. In claiming back some good from the evil of 11 September, Blair called for 'above all justice and prosperity for the poor and dispossessed, so that people everywhere can see the chance of a better future through the hard work and creative power of the citizen, not the violence and savagery of the fanatic'.

It is the global ideal of social democracy. It is also an extraordinarily high aim, one that can be achieved only by a re-dedication of the left's purpose on a global level. The political sphere must be engaged, and engaged more fully, in order to pursue such global reform strategies successfully. Ultimately, it provides the only legitimate forum for tackling the knots of issues that now command national and public space. The centre-left has had a relatively easy ride on the health of global capitalism in the advanced states that its governments inherited in the 1990s – especially in the US and Britain. Before 11

September, that ride was becoming rockier. Now it is rougher still.

Such a global politics would crucially include – as its first sketch does – an international court in which criminals would be judged, thus building the rudiments of a global justice system. At the same time as Osama Bin Laden was identified as being behind the Manhattan and Pentagon attacks, another alleged mass murderer, Slobodan Milosevic, was on trial in The Hague. The current limits of such a project are very clear: the choice of criminals is highly arbitrary, limited to those who can be opposed and caught by the armed forces of rich states. There is no agreed global police force, outside of the armies of these states – whose actions remain highly contentious. Yet the painful construction of such institutions is what might, in time, ensure that the values we have seen outraged gain wider currency: a mere punishment cannot achieve this.

The effort to create a system of global governance is now unavoidable, if the twin challenges of the new global movements and the new global terrorism are to be answered. The challenge facing national governments, especially progressive ones, is to articulate an international political agenda that addresses the underlying concerns and inequalities that have fuelled the creation of the new movements.

Such a programme can be achieved only by democratically legitimated state action, because that is where politics currently finds its largest support. The pointers to such a project come from theories and experience involving different levels of national, regional and global organisations. It is the use of networks, as well as centres, of power. This agenda, which fuses in new ways what were historically domestic and foreign policies, must become intertwined with the effort to draw the US positively into a more interdependent world.

Progressive governments need to take steps beyond the state acting through an interest-based system of voluntary collaboration with other individual states. Their aim must be a more concerted and systematic form of joint governance, emphasising dignity, distribution and dialogue as part of its structure, and creating binding obligations between nations and regions of the world. It should aim to avoid hierarchical bureaucracies – the implicit model still used in achieving integration in Europe. It should adhere to international law, based on human rights. But if open dialogue really is part of its practice, it has to recognise the limits of the appeal of arguments based on rights that are seen exclusively as part of Western culture.

The centre-left, which was the dominant political force in rich states in the late 1990s, is no longer a rising tide. Social democratic governments have been replaced by those of the right (which include elements of the far right) in Austria, Italy and Norway. In the US, a centrist Democratic president has been replaced by a determinedly right-wing one. The transnational conversations initiated by the governments of the left – the so-called Third Way or progressive governance ideas – now lack their initial momentum.

Yet these ideas remain the best on offer. They operate in a series of tensions between the private (in both the individual and business senses) and the public, constantly mediating between them and suggesting new advances and forms of co-operation and compromise. Compromise, far from being the shame of politics, is in most cases its achievement. Now, however, there is a clear need to accelerate the pace of creating a global politics, as the relatively comfortable positions and projects of Third Way governance in a period of rising prosperity give way to a sharper, more straitened time. The alternative, already proposed by the right, is to retreat to a national security that, given the state the world is in, becomes more and more insecure. The left is impelled to the option of openness through fidelity to its own values, and a continuing belief that these can best answer human needs.

2. A world coming apart

In 1997, the American editor and writer Lewis Lapham wrote a witty essay[2] on the World Economic Forum, which meets every year in the elite ski resort of Davos in Switzerland. Before setting off, he had dined at a pricey New York restaurant with three managers of a successful hedge fund, 'who characterised the Davos meeting as a futile transfer of worthless platitudes. The action in New York City during the week in question might turn up something a helluva lot more interesting than snow, and who could afford the lost opportunity cost? Why bother to dress up the everyday cruelties of standard capitalist business practice with the rags of a Sunday conscience? To what purpose and to whose benefit? Who was anybody kidding?'

In Davos, Lapham met Dr Klaus Schwab, the creator, in 1971, of the World Economic Forum. Schwab told Lapham that he had wanted capitalists to interest themselves in the globe, and had been successful in stimulating a broader – if at first tentative – consciousness than a mere focus on the bottom line. By the 1990s, said Schwab, the Davosites had begun seriously to question their purpose on earth.

'He attributed the shift in emphasis,' Lapham wrote, 'to an awareness among the more thoughtful of the world's landlords that the global economy was a good deal more complicated than anybody had thought, and that *in the absence of a coherent argument from the socialist left*, even the most well-meaning corporate citizens found themselves marooned in a vacuum.'

From the mid-1990s, that vacuum began to fill. A movement appeared that had at least some of the forms, if few of the courtesies, of the socialist left. In July 2001, Schwab wrote in *Newsweek*

International[3] that the global institutions – such as the International Monetary Fund, the World Bank, the World Trade Organisation and the United Nations – were failing. 'I am deeply sceptical, at this point, that the institutions responsible for promoting world peace, financial stability, socio-economic development and the free flow of goods and services will ever again be able to address these challenges on their own ... power has shifted to new actors, from multinational companies to NGOs and activist individuals.'

Schwab was digesting the lessons of the most disastrous Davos in its three-decade, generally successful history. The WEF of January 2001 had attracted the wrath of the anti-globalisation movements, which fastened on it as a nest of super-exploiters, and tried to disrupt it as they had the WTO meeting in Seattle in 1999, the first high peak of their success. Most of the clashes with police and the subsequent arrests took place in Zurich, as the protesters tried to get to or get away from Davos. But the business and political leaders heard and saw the crowds of demonstrators held back from their meetings: the whiffs of tear gas cast a pall, especially over those who thought they were there to do good.

At the same time as members of the WEF were meeting in such unaccustomed discomfort, a rival gathering was taking place in a warm, relaxed, down-at-heel Latin city to the south of Brazil. The World Social Forum in Pôrto Alegre was being staged by a group of global movements, political parties and trade unions – their core being a mixture of French left intellectual and Brazilian socialist groups. The WSF was timed to clash with the WEF – a recognition that the latter forum had become, over the past decade, an increasingly powerful symbol of the closed ranks of world capital. The WSF was designed to become a beacon of hope for the wretched of the earth, and was presented in these terms.

The WSF's organisers took a position of cold contempt towards the WEF – ironically, an attitude akin to that of the three hedge-fund managers with whom Lapham had supped ('Who was anybody kidding?'). Bernard Cassen, the senior editor of the radical monthly *Le Monde Diplomatique* and one of the founders of the Attac anti-capitalist network – the main promoter of the Pôrto Alegre meeting – said: 'We have nothing to say to the people in Davos. We know what their line

is. We know what they mean by global responsibility. It is press relations. This [the WSF] is an attempt to construct something quite different.'[4] Davos, however, did not respond in kind. It wanted to be
understood. It wanted dialogue. It proposed a debate, via a TV bridge,
between the two centres. After an argument among the main spon-
sors about the wisdom of being seen to treat with the devil, the Pôrto
Alegre camp agreed. It was a revealing experience.

Davos put up the most concerned people it had. They included the
administrator of the UN Development Programme, Mark Malloch
Brown, who was there to give a speech on corporate responsibility,
and the financier George Soros, who has spent many fortunes pump-
ing money into former communist states to assist the construction of
civil society, and has trenchant views on the downside of the global
capitalism through which he made his billions. They were active in
looking for solutions, but they seemed – at least from the flickering
screens in Pôrto Alegre – to be part of the problem. They also seemed
to belie Cassen's point that global capital was good at public relations.
Davos had fielded formally dressed, middle-aged white men: any TV
producer could have told them that, these days, it doesn't help to have
middle-aged white men making your case.

The Pôrto Alegre camp, by contrast, had an audience in which men
and women were fairly equally represented, and in which there was a
mixture of black, brown and white skins, clothed casually or gor-
geously. Walden Bello, a Filipino academic and trade activist, looked
and sounded as if he spoke for a movement when he told the Davos
representatives: 'We live on different planets. Here in Pôrto Alegre, we
are looking for ways of saving the world: you in Davos are looking for
ways of maintaining the hegemony of multinationals across the
world.' The Davos men, all of them chosen for their emollience and
even partial agreement with those in Pôrto Alegre, protested their
desire for improvements. But they did so against evidence of despera-
tion in Africa, multinational exploitation in Asia, failure of economic
reform in eastern Europe, widening inequalities everywhere. They did
so as the symbolism of their presentations screamed exclusiveness on
the Swiss side and inclusion on the Brazilian.

Pôrto Alegre was a ragbag of declamation, hot air and vapidity,
mixed with a few thoughtful talks that attempted to grapple with

realities. Its bravura moments were denunciations – usually of the US, or neoliberalism, or capitalist globalisation, or all of these. But unlike Davos, it sounded sure of itself. It had a moral wind in its sails.

That is the success of the global movements as a whole. They confront liberal-corporate uncertainty with radical assurance. They adopt the wretched of the earth, indeed the earth itself, as their cause, explicitly or implicitly consigning the task of destroying the planet to multinationals, global institutions and national governments. In eliciting a varied and often apologetic, guilty or concerned response from their opponents, they are able to bolster their own position ('even George Soros admits . . .'). The sheer range of the movements means that many respectable groups that have had structured dialogue with corporations, governments and international institutions – for example, Friends of the Earth and Greenpeace – have been wooed, wittingly or unwittingly, into being comrades-of-the-street with groups that throw rocks through Starbucks windows, carry banners saying 'Fuck Capitalism' and try to smash, and have been smashed by, the police.

The causes embraced by the movements include opposition to: global warming; the destruction of the ozone layer; the denial of modern and affordable medicines to the ailing of the third world; the cruelty practised on animals in medical and other experiments; the cruelty imposed on animals raised for their meat; the exploitation of third world labour by Western-based multinationals; the homogenisation of food and drink by the spread of such chains as McDonald's, Pizza Hut and Starbucks; the pushing of small/peasant farmers into ruin by the industrialisation of farming imposed by these fast-food chains and the supermarkets; the destruction of national or indigenous cultures by the sheer power and wealth of the (largely) US entertainment industries; the numbing effects of these entertainment and news media, serving to deceive or to narcotise; the sexual rigidity and homophobia of the political classes, discriminating against, or encouraging or allowing the mistreatment of, gay men and women; the covert or overt racism of these classes, desperate to keep the waves of dark-skinned people out of their wealthy enclaves; the vast sales and murderous potential of the (largely US or European) arms industries; the nuclear arsenals held by the 'old' nuclear weapons states, and the burgeoning proliferation of the new nuclear powers, such as

China, India and Pakistan; the corruption, vapidity and mendacity of modern politicians, in hock to corporate interests; the hypocrisy of modern liberalism-cum-social democracy, legitimating neo-imperial invasions in the name of humanitarian intervention and diminishing workers' rights in the name of full employment and competitiveness; and, above all else, the pauperisation of the developing world, with leaping gaps between the rich and poor, the haves and have-nots, both within and between states. These are merely some of the global issues. On the local level, to which these movements easily connect through the internet and local activists, there is much, much more.

Good-hearted people could see and hear a great deal in Pôrto Alegre – beneath the posturing – that would incline them to agree that here were 'different planets', and that they should land on the Pôrto Alegre one.

Globalisation is 'them': the emergence of a new grand narrative
Since the end of the cold war, a number of 'grand narratives' have been proposed as ways of understanding the world. These include:

- that ideological struggle had been replaced with a recognition that liberal democratic polities and market economics constituted the only grand system or ideology on offer[5];
- that globalisation was rendering national states increasingly powerless[6];
- that, on the contrary, states remained as powerful as ever and continued to seek to maximise their power and to protect themselves from other states doing the same[7];
- that the clash of ideologies had been replaced with a clash of civilisations, where cultural, religious and ethnic bonds reasserted themselves to bind nations and peoples together in civilisational blocs[8].

These narratives are not, of course, wholly mutually exclusive.

The collective view of the new global movements must now rank as another, if multi-authored, grand narrative. It is separate from that of the groups and states which take an avowedly anti-West/anti-American posture and which, at the extreme, have shown themselves willing to use terrorism against Western targets. But it shares some assumptions – especially the belief that globalisation is essentially Western/American capitalism, which is an oppressive and impoverishing force, and that American, and to a lesser extent Western, economic and foreign policies dominate and discriminate throughout the world.

This narrative has the advantage of making few recommendations as to the political, or institutional, strategies that might further the movements' aims. It operates on an idealist plane, far above the political world it opposes. Consciously or unconsciously, this separation of ideals from any coherent arrangements that might further them acts as a prophylactic for the movements: their approach cannot be opposed, because to do so is to oppose virtue. Unlike communism, which sought power, the core of the global movements' narrative is oppositional, and must remain so. It is also negative: it defines itself in opposition to the hegemony of the US, and its brand of capitalism.

The major moral plank of the global movements, one with which there is broad – if passive – public agreement, is that most of the world's people live in what we in the West consider misery. More than this – perhaps as important politically – an increased number of the very poor know their state in a way they did not when they were peasants. Industrialisation, urbanisation and now globalisation are powerful and rapid creators of a modern self-consciousness, and thus of modern grievance, which often turns towards the West to curse.

The charge: poverty, misery and exploitation in the world

Around three-quarters of the world's people live in what developed countries would classify as poverty. Half of the global population – roughly 3 billion people – live in abject poverty; nearly half of these – 1.2 billion in 2000 – live in utter destitution, on less than $1 a day, in danger of death by starvation or a related disease. Access to safe drinking water is unknown to 1 billion people; 2.4 billion have no adequate sanitation.

Children are brutalised by poverty: 250 million must work, sometimes ruining their constitution before adulthood. Of these, roughly 100 million find what work and shelter they can on the streets; the same number have no schooling whatsoever. More than 1 million girls under the age of 18 are forced into prostitution; a further 300,000 children are 'enlisted' in armies, militias and guerrilla groups.

The poor countries are tremendously burdened with diseases, for which they have few remedies. Malaria, measles, tetanus, syphilis and diarrhoeal diseases, some barely known in developed countries, are rampant. AIDS, in particular, is devastating sub-Saharan Africa: of the 35 million sufferers worldwide, 24 million live in the subcontinent.

The rich world also has large pockets of (relative) poverty, which have defied economic upturns. In the countries belonging to the Organisation for Economic Co-operation and Development – roughly speaking, the developed states – 8 million people suffer from malnutrition. In the world's richest country, the US, 40 million have no health insurance and 20 per cent of the population is functionally illiterate.

All rich countries have a growing underclass of workers and jobless whose skills have not kept pace with rapid technological changes. In European states, the percentage of those living below the poverty line, as defined by the rich world, varies from less than 10 per cent in Scandinavia, through 15-20 per cent in Germany and France, to 20–25 per cent in Italy, Spain and the UK. The problem is much worse in countries that entered global modernity with an antiquated industrial structure clanking behind them – in the former Soviet bloc, for example.

Inequality is growing sharply: even where the poor are getting richer, the rich are getting richer much more quickly. When, nearly 200 years ago, average yearly global income was around $650 (in today's prices), the differential between the richest and poorest countries was around 3:1. The development of the West produced vast inequalities in the latter half of the 19th and the first half of the 20th centuries: by 1950, the ratio was 35:1. By 1973, it was 44:1, and now it is around 75:1. Inequality has also tended to rise within countries – in the 1980s and early 1990s, by between 15 and 20 per cent in countries as diverse as Sweden, the UK and the US. In Russia in the 1990s, after the collapse of communism, inequality doubled.

Around two-thirds of the world's population accounts for only one-fifth of foreign trade, receives one-tenth of total foreign direct investment and generates only a quarter of its GDP. 'On the extreme margins of globalisation,' writes David Reynolds, 'was the international underclass of heavily indebted poor countries, constituting nearly one-quarter of World Bank members. These 41 states (32 of them in sub-Saharan Africa) owed debts amounting to more than double their export earnings. By the 1990s, thanks to the burdens of debt servicing, developing countries were transferring more money to the IMF and the World Bank than they received.'[9]

Three of the four elements – earth, water and air – are said to be in deep crisis. The earth had defied neo-Malthusian forecasts of overpopulation in the late 20th century by increasing its grain yield to a peak of 763 pounds per person in 1984. But that fell to 690 pounds by 1996. Water had become scarce in many of the countries that needed it most, as water tables fell and irrigation systems did not grow in tune with populations – or in some countries, as in Central Asia, actually decayed from a lack of investment. The air, cleaner in some developed urban centres, grew much fouler in the teeming cities of the developing world, where pollution controls were weak or ignored: roughly 1.3 billion people breathed in disease every day, in the streets and in their homes.

Two themes were particularly troublesome. The 'hole in the ozone layer', apparently caused by the release of chlorofluorocarbons into the atmosphere, meant that the protection against solar radiation was reduced, with potentially serious consequences of diminishing fish stocks and skin cancers. The 'greenhouse effect', or global warming, was brought about by the release of carbon dioxide and other gasses (including chlorofluorocarbons), and was believed to cause melting of the ice caps and raising of the sea level to the point where coastal cities and arable land would be threatened. The effects of these would be more disastrous for poorer countries – such as low-lying Bangladesh – than for the rich. Even if they escape direct effects, the increased cost of essential supplies would hit them hardest.

Civil rights tend to diminish in rough – but far from automatic – equivalence with the poverty of the states in question: in some of the poorest African countries, with almost no effective government, the most basic rights have no guarantor beyond group strength. In the conflicts unleashed after the collapse of communism – in former Yugoslavia, in the former Soviet Caucasian states and in Chechnya – civil war has rubbed out any civil protection in the areas of fighting. The poor in large parts of Asia, Latin America and the Middle East are often at the mercy of local or national warlords, or drug lords, or landlords.

This is a basic model of the charge sheet made by both non-governmental organisations and, more insistently, the global movements. It represents a kind of truth: it is certain that a majority of people in the world live below, often far below, the material level of the West – including the poor in the West. But three things are missing from the above account, and are usually missing from the accounts that the global movements give of the world.

First, they rarely reflect the considerable debate that usually attends statistics – particularly statistics about health and the environment. Second, the picture is static. It does not show improvements. The material position of many developing countries, especially China and India, has improved substantially over the past decade – even where, as in some Latin American states, the improvement is followed by setbacks. Third, it does not deal with the see-saws of experience – for example, in the case of individuals and families wrenched, or wrenching themselves, out of rural areas into cities, whereby the drudgery of village life, where it is almost impossible to improve one's chances, is replaced by the poverty of city life. That poverty may be deeper, but there might be chances for improvement; and the political leverage of the urban poor is generally greater than that of the rural poor.

For NGOs, a concentration on the facts of poverty is a matter of continuing to tap the charity of the rich world. In the case of the global movements, that same concentration is a political strategy: to demonstrate the inability of capitalism, rich states and the institutions and programmes they have created, to address the issue. Whether the world as a whole is getting better or worse is another discussion, but it is crucial to note that an account of misery cannot be complete unless it is made both relative and dynamic, and unless some measure is taken of different accounts of the severity of crises.

The pillars of society: accusing the West's institutions

A view of the world as riven between rich and poor has fuelled campaigns by the older global movements for decades, and by socialist and Christian groups for more than a century. But in the 1990s, the new global movements introduced a harsher and much more aggressive approach, which holds that the institutions – including democratic institutions – of both the developed and the developing world are not ameliorating the world's ills, but deepening its problems. This marks not just an extension of the global critique, but also a new dimension to it: one where all the world's political and economic relationships are seen as failing. The power of the new movements lies partly in their claim that these relationships are acting systematically to dispossess part of the world's population. The standard pragmatic liberal/centre-left response that 'the world is as it is, but we are doing what we can with what we've got' seems weak in comparison.

In this, the argument between social democracy and communism is reproduced: the centre-left is seen as in thrall to capital, weak-kneed, spineless. But there is a central difference. Communism held itself up as an antidote. Now there is the critique without the antidote – an advantage for the global movements. They are not forced to recognise the failings of any actually existing model of society that they are promoting – one of the factors that killed communism.

The global movements have moved to the position they hold through amplifying critiques long deployed on both the left and, to a lesser extent, the right; and by benefiting from crises, or perceived crises, of most of the institutions that support Western societies. These allow the movements to paint such societies as corrupt, indifferent and deceitful. These critiques capitalise on a range of dissatisfactions and suspicions that are no longer mobilised mainly on party lines – indeed, that are increasingly expressed in terms of disillusionment with 'conventional' party politics, of the right or the left. This is often amplified by media that are more willing to be harshly critical of government and other institutions, and by a public temper that, increasingly less bound by loyalty to party or traditional views, can be more easily swung – if temporarily – behind a movement aimed at politicians, bureaucrats, officials or bosses.

The 'failed' world of reformism

The new movements are particularly critical of the international financial institutions (IFIs) – the International Monetary Fund (IMF) and the World Bank, together with the Organisation for Economic Co-operation and Development (OECD), the Group of Seven (Eight with Russia in the political forum), the European Union, the North American Free Trade Area (Nafta) and, above all, the World Trade Organisation (WTO). Indeed, the anti-globalisation activists' largest threat may be their efforts to destroy the legitimacy of these global institutions, now in their critical middle age.

The international financial institutions were created with explicitly – and by past standards radically – reformist goals. An open trading system, ensured by the IMF and the World Bank, was held to be the best antidote against the kind of war from which much of the world had just emerged. John Maynard Keynes, the British economist who was the most important theorist behind the creation of the international bodies, and who was a senior UK representative at the Bretton Woods conference that established the bodies, described the Bank's mandate as post-war reconstruction and then the development of poor countries. But what was seen, half a century ago, as conducive to peace and the relief of poverty is now seen as precisely the opposite.

The attacks on these institutions mark a sharp break with the idealism, largely a social democratic idealism, of previous generations. In this, they accord with the critique that the communist world levelled at the Western post-war economic settlement. The global movements are alert to the injection of neoliberal ideology and practice into the strategies of the IFIs in the last two decades of the 20th century. They see it as a deliberate step to ensure the wealth of a quarter of the world's population through the impoverishment of the remaining three-quarters. Whatever credibility the international financial and trading institutions might have had in the eyes of the radical left, they lost it when they adopted mechanisms such as structural adjustment strategies for developing countries as prerequisites for granting aid through IMF and World Bank programmes.

The shift to structural adjustment coincided with the victory of capitalism over the alternative attempt at a world system. Thus the doctrine of modernisation through structural adjustment became bound up with the view that a global liberal democratic-capitalist hegemony heralded the end of history. This gave structural adjustment the appearance of a new ideological consensus, when in fact it was largely a response to the failures of other institutional approaches to modernisation tried by the international bodies in the recent past.

Of all the global institutions that are seen to serve the dominant interests, the most contentious is the WTO, the successor to the General Agreement on Tariffs and Trade. Free trade – which is one of the pillars of the Washington consensus urged on developing countries – is seen almost as a proxy for the rich world's despoliation of the poor. That is also because the world trade agenda rapidly became so much more ambitious in the 1980s. The Uruguay round, which culminated in 1994 with a treaty that created the WTO from the Gatt, hugely increased the scope of trade rules – with new agreements on services, investments, intellectual property, sanitary measures, plant health and technical barriers to trade (rather than a concentration on formal tariff barriers, as had been the practice since the Gatt was set up in 1947). Agriculture and textiles, which had enjoyed very high protection in many countries, were brought into the Gatt/WTO rules for the first time. The disputes system became more interventionist. Unlike the Gatt, which was a Cinderella among the much larger and more visible international institutions that emerged from Bretton Woods, the WTO rapidly became a major and contentious player. Its 50th anniversary celebrations in Geneva, two years before the Seattle event, attracted a crowd of demonstrators – a few of whom, harbin gers of larger skirmishes to come, threw stones and bottles, and later set fire to cars. 'God is dead,' read one of their placards. 'The WTO has replaced him.'

The conviction that the IFIs' advice was counterproductive, perhaps even deliberately, was boosted by the experience of the former states of the Soviet Union. With the exception of the three small Baltic states of Estonia, Latvia and Lithuania, economic collapse has continued for years after the collapse of communism. For Russia, the 1990s were very negative years, with a loss (according to official figures) of 50 per cent of output, a plunge in living standards and a huge increase in crime, disease and inequality. Worse happened in Ukraine, where the industrial structure was proportionately even more skewed and the efforts at reform weaker. The Central Asian states, largely dependent on a Soviet system of allocation and demand, were impoverished: the weakest, such as Kirghizia and Tajikistan, are destitute. The three

Caucasian states of Armenia, Azerbaijan and Georgia fell into civil war. All of these states had IMF and World Bank programmes; in none did they seem to work. At the same time, however, the political and financial elites who generally supported the programmes enriched themselves. In some cases – particularly in Central Asia – the rulers became more openly despotic than they had been in the late Soviet era. The conclusion was obvious: the structural adjustment recommended by the IFIs, and put into place by the liberal reformers in the Russian and other governments, was to blame.

The global godfathers: crime and corruption in the network society

Crime and corruption have billowed in both the developing and the developed world, and are seen by the global movements as the creation, or at least by-products, of global capitalism. Corruption is ingrained in the governments of many states – including the world's largest, such as China, India, the Philippines and Russia. It cripples African administrations, where government, especially supreme power, is regarded as the surest way to wealth. Corruption in poor and developing countries is not a marginal economic matter: it can drain away very large parts of exiguous revenues and, because of its use as a source of rewards for supporters, it destroys initiatives to build up a neutral state apparatus. Linked to this, deepening their hold on many societies, are growing global crime networks, which touch political corruption on the one hand and international terrorism on the other, requiring both for their expansion and efficiency. In 1994, the UN reported: 'Organised transnational crime, with the capacity to expand its activities and target the security and economies of countries, in particular developing ones and economies in transition, represents one of the major threats that governments have to deal with in order to ensure their stability, the safety of their people, the preservation of the whole fabric of their society and the viability and further development of their economies.'[10]

The drugs trade is one of the largest sources of revenue; the trade in immigrants is growing to match it; a trade in body parts is a new area of profit; prostitution and children-for-adoption networks are blooming on a transnational basis. And there are other sinister instances of trafficking, such as that of chemical, biological and nuclear materials for terrorist groups. 'State sovereignty,' writes Manuel Castells, 'already battered by the processes of globalisation and identification, is directly threatened by flexible networks of crime that bypass controls and assume a level of risk that no other organisations are capable of absorbing. The collective fascination of the entire planet with action movies where the protagonists are the players in organised crime may well indicate the cultural breakdown of traditional moral order and the implicit recognition of a new society, made up of communal identity and unruly competition, of which global crime is a condensed expression.'[11] Globalisation is seen as responsible for what Castells calls 'unruly competition': a world in which commodities, of which a whole world is made conscious through the media, become global objects of desire, which in poor societies can be quickly acquired only through crime.

All in it for themselves: business, politics and corruption

Political leadership in the developed world is seen, where not straightforwardly corrupt, as deeply compromised. Though corruption is a much less decisive factor in the governance of richer societies, they are subject to periodic scandals. These have diluted the trust of a public that overlooked, or was not informed about, similar or worse delinquency on the part of the elite in previous decades. The Clinton administration was accused of a series of funding scandals; though many were unproven, they showed at best a willingness to turn the mystique of the presidency and the White House into a superior theme park. Currently, the close links between business and the Bush administration make objectivity and distance hard to claim. A Greenpeace postcard, published while this essay was being written, featured on its front 'The Bush/Cheney Energy Cocktail' – with oil, nuclear waste and lumps of coal being emptied into a cocktail glass; on the reverse side, Greenpeace explained that 'The Bush/Cheney Energy Plan is an energy "scam" – a payback to the oil, coal and nuclear interests who helped fund the Bush/Cheney election campaign'.

Corruption is now routinely portrayed as endemic in the political systems of other rich countries. In France, allegations of serious financial irregularities have been made against figures on the left – such as Dominique Strauss Kahn, the former finance minister – and on the right, including the president, Jacques Chirac. In Italy, which enjoyed relatively corruption-free years in the late 1990s, the new prime minister of the right-wing alliance, Silvio Berlusconi, took office with a pyramid of cases against him, which included the accusation of close links with the Mafia. Even if all the allegations were proved false (one of the most important charges – that his company Mediaset bribed the financial police – was dismissed by an appeal court in October 2001), his ownership of the commercial half of Italian broadcasting and his political control of the other, state-held half made him the first democratically elected leader to hold such formidable power of persuasion. It was a point insistently made by protesters at the G8 summit in Genoa in July 2001 when a young *carabiniere* shot dead an activist, Carlo Giuliani, who was stoning his car.

Even in countries with relatively little corruption – such as the UK – the links that politicians of the left and right forge with business in order to raise money for increasingly expensive party administration and campaigns raise questions of influence and transparency. A well-publicised example was over a donation of £1m from the head of Formula One to the Labour Party, which, in government, exempted the sport from a ban on tobacco sponsorship and advertising. And a donation to the Millennium Dome from the Hinduja brothers, Indian businessmen under investigation for corruption in their own country, became controversial when they rapidly received British citizenship. At the very least, such cases undermine the ability of democratic Western governments to preach particular forms of development and institutional practice to other parts of the world.

In these and other instances in which ministers asserted their own good intentions and actions, the assumption on the part of radicals – and many non-radicals – was that government was in the hands of corporations and wealthy individuals, who manipulated it at will. Given that the walls separating political parties (especially those of the left) from major private funding crumbled soon after the Berlin Wall did, the charge was almost certain to have some substance somewhere, sometime. Anti-globalisation activists use such instances to prove that governments and states have become indistinguishable passengers on the gravy train – with the politicians supinely doing the global capitalists' bidding, providing false democratic cover for legitimating their business strategies. On the 'March against neoliberalism' that was the high point of the Pôrto Alegre gathering, the most popular poster showed senior members of the Brazilian government as helpless dupes of US corporations.

Not unto us, O Lord: the new militancy of organised religion

The world's ethical moorings are everywhere becoming less solid. Postmodern thinking in its various forms produced the impression that gone were the pragmatic verities by which people believed their lives were led. 'We live in a world of signs without fault, without truth and without origin,' wrote the French philosopher Jacques Derrida. Activists in the 1980s and 1990s seized upon such insights as proof that life was meaningless, or at least that it had meaning not contained in the workaday secularism of modern consumer society.

The series of rapid breakthroughs in gene sequencing, biotechnology, transplant surgery and embryo research raised vast and unresolved – unresolvable, perhaps – questions about the nature of human-ness and animal-ness; the limits of interference in human reproduction, and the consequences of genetic readouts of each human being which might predict illnesses or death. These increasingly presented governments of rich states with decisions along two conflicting axes: a strongly or vaguely held moral distaste for meddling in 'natural' processes on the one hand, and the scientific-medical-commercial push to improve human welfare and to develop new products on the other. Governments and companies stood accused of entering into the most intimate human activities with an eye for profit and prestige.

These dilemmas and ethical challenges, too complex for many to grasp and apparently beyond the scope of existing ethical practices and Western institutions, have contributed to a wider sense of disengagement and uncertainty about the efficacy and legitimacy of public institutions. Within polities, all politicians are engaged in an increasingly desperate struggle to demonstrate to their electorates that they can effect positive change in the world around them.

At the same time, the world's religious traditions have suffered a kind of bifurcation. On the one hand, they have been prey to various fundamentalisms – Orthodox Judaism, radical Islam, or Moral Majority-type Christian evangelism. Even in the post-war Catholic

Church, which had been moderate, a charismatic Pope John Paul II attempted a re-dogmatisation, setting himself against what most Catholics practised – such as birth control and accepting Protestantism as an equally valid faith. Hinduism, generally seen as a byword for tolerance, received an injection of radical sectarianism from the ideologists of the Rashtriya Swayamsevak Sangh (RSS), the organisation that provides the ideological glue for India's government, led by the Hindu nationalist Bharatiya Janata Party. Orthodox Judaism, in some of its manifestations, provided the most extreme support for the policy of settlements in Palestine.

All of these religious movements have had an overtly, and generally radical, political programme and have sought hegemony, or at least strong influence, over the governments and parties to which they are close. They vary in how much they have achieved, and in some countries, notably Iran, radical Islam appears to be retreating in the face of a movement among clerics and politicians seeking a greater distance between the religion and the state. But in other parts of the Islamic world, clerics join with political figures to mould minds, not to love God so much as to hate the West, claiming that the first demands the second. Karen Armstrong has made the argument[12] that religious fundamentalism is a response to the conditions of economic and social modernisation in which the moderate and established forms of religion, once secure in tradition, decline as these traditions are destroyed, rather than being allowed to evolve. The emergence of radical religious groupings can thus be understood partly as a reaction to the wider conditions in which the West's economic supremacy has been reasserted – a systemic reaction, in other words, not an incomprehensible shift towards fanaticism.

On the other hand, where religion has opened itself to liberal, humanist currents, forsworn any direct influence on the state and stressed its social and therapeutic role, it has declined. In spite of Pope John Paul II's best efforts, Catholicism became a minority practice even in its Western European heartlands of France, Ireland, Italy and Spain. It was bested in Latin America by charismatic evangelism. The Protestant world's churches have lost congregations, except where they became evangelist. By the turn of the millennium, both the Anglican Archbishop of Canterbury, Dr George Carey, and the head of the Catholic Church in England and Wales, Cardinal Cormac Murphy-O'Connor, were warning of a complete collapse of Christianity in the UK.

For most rich states, increased scepticism and a decline in the power of religion over the state have been welcome, meaning diminished intolerance towards minority faiths. But the decline of moderate religions has given radical faiths and movements more legitimacy, and deepened conflict. Moderate faith had operated – and still does for some – as a standard of decency and restraint; now these civilising tasks have been implicitly devolved to the state, and its education and criminal justice systems. If Carey and O'Connor are right, we are about to find out what the end of observance means in a state that still depends on established Christianity for its self-definition and for the contours of its landscapes and cityscapes.

Tradition and 'the natural way of doing things' – as Ulrich Beck and Anthony Giddens write[13] – no longer work in developed societies, and increasingly don't in developing ones, either. We in the rich societies live among the ruins of great corporate moral codes, which still protect us from the worst of the modern tempest, but no longer have walls thick or intact enough to restrain us from going out to do our own, individual things. Respect or fear – which had been accorded to churches, governments and professional institutions – have weakened, sometimes to vanishing point. The dilemma for tradition is not simply that people's behaviour cannot be controlled as it once was. It is more often the case that the new risks and dilemmas seem too complex to be answered by the traditional codes. At the same time, the global shifts in power have meant that national governments cannot control what they did, while no governments or elected assemblies control, or even regulate, the global economy and polity. That is where the chasm yawns, and where the new movements situate themselves.

The dollar almighty: the new power of corporations

Companies had long laboured under a sentiment that saw them as exploitative, indifferent to workers and producing large wealth for their top executives and shareholders. The collapse of communism and socialism seemed, at first, to have ended that obloquy. The old critique has been amplified in the past decade, at the same time as the prevailing form of capitalism has become more focused on profits, shareholder value and efficiency. Corporations, it was believed by many, had left behind the early post-war period of corporate stability. Whereas they once offered more or less secure employment – sometimes for life – to workers at every level, now people were hired on the basis of their short-term usefulness to the corporation, and were let go as quickly. For the unskilled or single-skilled, working life could be particularly harsh: they were always at risk of being replaced by automated equipment and consigned to a service sector that, though plentiful in jobs, was very low-paid at the unskilled end.

In developing countries, business had a dual existence and image. As foreign direct investment became more and more important to states' economies, it was wooed ardently by governments and development corporations. As Ulrich Beck has observed, the power companies now have is not that of 'invading' a country, but of withholding an invasion: 'not controlling but the disdaining to control is what threatens national society and the nation state. States yearn for nothing so much as the invasion of investors, and fear nothing so much as their retreat.'[14] The withholding of invasion has been particularly marked in sub-Saharan Africa and in much of the former Soviet Union: it does not make capitalism more popular.

The corporations themselves, though they spent large sums on public relations to burnish their image, were not models of egalitarian practice. The gulf between the cleaner and the chief executive has, over the past two decades, grown much greater. Successful chief executives – or even unsuccessful ones – would, through salaries, stock options and bonuses, become millionaires in a year, multimillionaires in five years. Young men and women in the great financial and investment centres would receive salaries deep into six figures (in dollars or pounds), often for performing functions that few could understand, or see as productive. This was particularly the case in the US throughout the 1980s and 1990s, when working-class, even middle-class, incomes were stagnating. All over the developed world, and in privileged enclaves in the developing one, those who had mastered the new business and financial universe went on a long, rich roll.

The message is the problem: entertainment, sensation and the media

The media were increasingly described – and not just by radicals – as part of the problem, not the provider of either an answer or even a decent sort of question. The media came to be seen as merely another branch of business – the branch that justifies the rule of business itself. Its public service ethic, where it is or was professed, is regarded as a mere fig leaf for self-interest. In the 1990s, there was a consolidation of news and entertainment into a few, largely US corporations that sprawled across TV and radio, newspapers and magazines, film production and theme parks, distribution and cinema chains, video outlets and music studios, internet service providers and public relations companies.

These interests make up what the media consultant Michael J Wolf calls 'the entertainment economy', in which entertainment, including news and analysis of the world in which we live, is packaged to encourage increased consumption: 'entertainment has become a key differentiator in virtually every aspect of the broader consumer economy . . . in choosing where to buy french fries, how we relate to political candidates, what airline we want to fly, what pyjamas we choose for our kids and which mall we want to buy them in, entertainment is increasingly influencing every one of these choices that each of us makes every day'.[15] That this exceptionally powerful series of conglomerates should now be in command of most of the information we receive is increasingly considered to narrow, rather than broaden, the possibilities for independent analysis and thought.

Media power has created much of what is most obvious to us in globalisation. In some interpretations[16], globalisation is the process of integrating communications infrastructure, dating back to the telegraph in 1879. But, perhaps because they are the organisations whose activities link together all other identities and organisations, and which span sectors and countries, the media have an ungovernable quality, resisting definition, operating through decentralised activities that make regulation or censorship increasingly difficult. Yet at the same time, they centralise power through mergers and takeovers into huge blocs of economic and political influence, which often seem to stand above and beyond the political institutions that are supposed to govern them. As Jane Stokes and Anna Reading have observed: 'The effective exercise of political power to secure cultural sovereignty [is] more and more difficult to achieve.'[17]

News events themselves increasingly partake of the spectacular – such as the O J Simpson trial or the Monica Lewinsky affair. Ironically, one effect of the intense competition for audience share has been to produce news and current affairs coverage that is – by past standards – ultra combative, borrowing from radical journalism an in-your-face approach to politicians and a steady concentration on their personal lives and public disasters. This shift in coverage accorded well with the radicalism of the new global movements, who had the luxury of both condemning the media for being conformist and hearing their own views underpinned by the media's news output.

The world's politics and conflicts are increasingly played out through network media. Both the bitterly contested demonstrations in Genoa in July 2001 and the attacks on the World Trade Towers on 11 September were designed, in part, as televisual events. The media's role in exacerbating or resolving conflicts, however, never seems to become any clearer.

The state we're losing: government and parties under threat

The state no longer functions as it did for a large part of the 20th century – as a provider of services, a producer of essential goods, a protector of the national honour in wars and a focus of the citizen's devotion. It has not lost all of these functions; in wealthy states, the role of taxation has tended to rise rather than fall, in order to fund increasing transfer payments. It remains the primary international actor: transnational institutions take their legitimacy from states, rather than vice versa.

But the last decades of the 20th century appeared to mark the end of a period in which dependence on the state was encouraged. The long era of peace after the Second World War has gradually relieved the state of what was, for centuries, a principal task: defence and the waging of war. Its old hierarchies are diminishing, its mystique is now mocked, its secrets hard to protect from demands of openness. It must share power at every level: downwards, as the centralised states respond to pressures to devolve authority; and upwards, as international institutions, regional groupings and, in Europe, a Union that is developing an increasing number of state-like functions, claim more and more authority.

The voluntary bodies that were organised to provide governance of the state – political parties – are in a much more serious position. They are declining in membership, especially of the young. One of the great and best organised parties in the world, Germany's Social Democrats, lost 200,000 members out of a million in the last years of the 20th century: of the remainder, fewer than 40,000 were under 35.

Parties are not considered part of modern life by the young: their hierarchical organisation is off-putting, and is made worse by the way those at the top – the party leaders – listen less and less to members. The weakness of the state, and the limits it has in responding to pressures and crises, rebound on the parties: why join a party whose limits are those of a limited state? For the left, the abandonment of socialism has deprived parties of a goal that, although it may never have been attained or attainable, gave its gatherings a sense of ethical purpose transcending the workaday civilities (or incivilities) and duties of party life. Like other voluntary associations, they succumb to indifference, individual privatisation and television.

Many of the pillars, old and new, of the world are either shifting or crumbling. The good life (for individuals) is increasingly seen as an end in itself in the rich states: hope of it is both the opium and the lash of the poor in all states, developed and developing. However, that is open to two fundamental objections by the new global movements. First, and most obviously, that the good life is not coming to the majority of the world's population anytime soon. Second – these movements claim its possession is at best a selfish luxury on the part of the Western middle classes, at worst the condition of the poverty of all the rest. The stage is set for a new version of the 19th- and 20th-century politico-morality play – only, this time, acted out on a global stage.

3. The global movements and their beliefs

The global movements did not come 'out of nowhere'. They have a history. An important stimulus to their growth was official: it came from the development of the international organisations created after the Second World War at Bretton Woods, and the establishment of the UN. From the 1950s, Christian and other groups drew on the developmental ideology and their own beliefs to create organisations that sought to give substance to the aims of alleviating poverty, defending human rights, protecting the environment and assisting impoverished and/or abused women and children.

The revolutionary or Marxist left was not very interested in these organisations, except to denounce them for their reformism. But social democrats saw in these bodies – such as Oxfam, Save the Children, Christian Aid and Médecins sans Frontières – an outlet for their idealism and ideas, and many leftists were active and influential within them. Governments began to use them as conduits for aid policies, as they were more efficient, knowledgeable and honest than either their own bureaucracies or private contractors. By 1990, more than a quarter of development aid was routed through the NGOs.

In the 1990s, the development movement grew exponentially; again, the largest stimulus was official. The UN began a series of major conferences on global issues: at the first of these, on the environment in 1992, the event's general secretary, the Canadian Maurice Strong, allowed all interested NGOs to participate. Roberto Savio, chairman of the Rome-based news agency Interpress, wrote that 'at a conference where the majority of the delegates were diplomats operating according to the instructions of their governments, and frequently without any emotional involvement in their actions, the arrival of a sea of people with passions and deeply held commitments upset the traditional mechanism of diplomatic consensus'.[18]

This description points again to an image that has greatly assisted the global movements: the apparently dramatic difference between the passionate, engaged activists and the bloodless diplomats; between those who wish to move the hearts and minds of the world, and those who simply go through the motions. In a world whose media increasingly privilege emotive over intellectual responses, which is more attractive?

Savio also pointed out an unintended consequence of the NGOs' involvement, and a contributory factor to their much greater strength in the 1990s. 'The major conferences of the 1990s achieved the ideal objectives which they had set for themselves to a greater degree than had been thought possible; things reached the point where certain countries preferred to sign the final document even if they did not agree with it, in order to avoid negative fallout in terms of their image. Naturally, they would later take steps to avoid the actual implementation of the document.' This inflation of rhetoric and commitment, coupled with the later evasion of these commitments, worked to the governments' disadvantage. Having put on record a promise to eradicate this and conquer that, the inevitable failure could reasonably be held against them as evidence of their lack of will.

This echoes a more general challenge facing national governments and politicians. They must win power through commanding, above all, television. To do so, they must be dramatic. Yet politics is increasingly a halting, uneven, issue-by-issue process that politicians must negotiate through a multitude of interest groups by means of the administrative machinery of the nation state – itself imperfect, thus raising endless problems of delivery. There is a large gulf between televised rhetoric and practical delivery.

A radicalisation that could capitalise on the 'insincerity' and 'hypocrisy' of politicians increasingly reaped rewards. The 1990s were a time when appeals to the developed world's conscience seemed to work best – partly because it was no longer atrophied by fighting world communism. President Bush Senior is remembered and mocked for foreseeing a new world order; it is less often remembered that he saw it as one in which a respect for and extension of human rights would be the main task. This was widely seen as hypocrisy, and Bush's record, especially as Ronald Reagan's vice-president in his dealings with Central and South America, supports that interpretation. But Bush was also sensing the way in which the wind was shifting, ultimately to blow him away.

The centre left gathered strength, then came to power in North America and later in Europe. Many members of these governments had been active in, or deeply influenced by, the radical movements of the 1960s. They made a point of espousing many agendas of the NGOs. Robin Cook, the first New Labour foreign secretary, announced in 1997 that the government would seek to add an ethical dimension to its foreign policy. A major part of that was an intense dialogue with NGOs such as Oxfam, Amnesty International and Saferworld, whose officials were on occasion seconded to the Foreign Office.

The NGOs had been admitted to the halls of power because they seemed to be the wave of the future; their growth in the 1980s had been extraordinary. Greenpeace, which began in 1972, had grown from 800,000 members in 1985 to nearly 2.5 million in 1990 – the largest membership of any environmental group ever, and this at a time when it was famous for its aggressive efforts to stop whaling or oil exploration. In the mid-1990s, several groups were formed to focus on the Multilateral Agreement on Investment (MAI), promoted by the OECD. The meetings on this accord, held behind closed doors, were targeted and charged with writing rules in favour of the rich countries at the behest of multinationals. There had already been divisions between nations on the accord, but the sudden and explosive opposition of the new groups seemed to deal the death blow. Almost all environmental groups underwent explosive growth during this period, while most political parties were shedding members at almost as rapid a rate. The idealists were leaving the hulks of political movements to the technocrats, spin-doctors and managers.

The new global movements were not just much more idealistic, imaginative, militant and glamorous than the parties: they also placed fewer demands on their supporters. Joining Greenpeace or Ya Basta! meant serving one's ideals by paying a subscription or attending an exciting demonstration. There were no local branches, no meetings, no membership life save that conducted through the mail or the e-mail. A fellow party member might live miles away in the same town or borough and be known to his colleagues through common work; a fellow Greenpeace member might live next door and be wholly unknown.

At the same time, the hollowing out of the left that deprived it of its coherence allowed a new militancy to emerge. The outstanding example is in the French peasant movement, whose figurehead is Jose Bové, one of the most prominent and iconic figures of the global movements. Bové was always a rebel. He objected to military service, went on the run from the police when he failed to get an exemption, and ended up a sheep farmer. He led a protest against the extension of military camps, and was a militant anti-nuclear campaigner.

His status grew when he expressed the opposition of small producers to the domination of agribusiness (a worldwide phenomenon); and when the US placed import bans on Roquefort cheese, in which the sheep farmers of Larzac specialised, he attracted national, then international, attention. His Confederation Paysanne was able to upstage the older farmers' and peasants' organisations, including those dominated by the Communist Party. Bové works in the modern manner, with direct action, broad support (especially from intellectual circles) and constant appearances in the mass media, which have responded with delight to his open, demotic style and his Asterix-like moustache. In 1999, supporters of his Confederation destroyed a building site for a McDonald's restaurant in Millau. The demonstration he mounted in the town in the summer of 2000 brought in the gamut of organisations, including Trotskyists, trade unions, Parisian intellectuals, local folklorists and Catholic groups.

In France, which has a consciously anti-American tradition on both left and right, he was seen as a hero – or at least as a necessary interlocutor – all the way to the top of a cohabitation government. He has met President Jacques Chirac and Prime Minister Lionel Jospin; significantly, he found more hostility on the 'old' left. The weekly *Nouvel Observateur* brought him face-to-face with Jean Glavany, the minister of agriculture – an encounter which clarified that Glavany, as a socialist, cleaved to 'progress, reason, knowledge – what do you want? I'm of the left!' Bové is not of that left at all: he cleaves to action, charisma and emotion.

In this, he is a model of the new movements, and a model of the new network society and politics. He is able to turn a local struggle into a global issue through the identification of an enemy – whether the global organisations that regulate trade, the US that dominates it or the capitalist companies (usually American, such as McDonald's) that are believed to ruin a natural or traditional or popular way of life. Bové, endowed with a natural talent for drama, a pleasant and patient demeanour, and a sense of how far to go, was one of the first 'leaders' of the new global movements.

That 'leader' is in quotation marks points to another important feature of the movements: they do not have leaders in the conventional sense – like governments have premiers, or businesses have chief executives. They have inspirers: people who, through their actions and their virtue, take on a position that is there to be copied and learnt from. This points up one of the greatest organisational, as well as ideological, strengths of the new global movements: they are networks that are decentralised and 'leaderless' by inclination. Their shared anti-materialist beliefs and common enemies in capitalism, corporate power and American hegemony allow them to work along a rich axis of protest in which the local is connected to the national, the national to the global. Almost anyone with a computer, some time and a passion for radical thought and action can do it: it is a network and an activity that gives meaning, purpose and moral certainty to the bolder spirits of a generation – a generation, moreover, across the globe.

That the movements are successful as leaderless entities also points to one of their most important weaknesses. They are not capable of creating structured ways of deploying resources and ordering priorities for action on a large scale over a prolonged period. That is, in their current forms, they do not offer a practical alternative to the way that hierarchical structures of governance currently try to order activity in the world around them. Their alternative can be offered only at the level of oppositional activism and political or rhetorical challenge – their actions are, in every sense, symbolic. This may help to explain why so many among this spectrum retain a strong, neo-Marxian belief that if the right conditions are created and the power structures challenged, then spontaneous new forms of order will emerge; and also why so many of the alternative social or economic models to which they point operate only on the micro scale. The evidence that they can operate spontaneously on a mass scale seems to be, at best, patchy.

The most thoughtful among their leading spirits understand this, and are trying to remedy it. In Italy, where the global movements are said to be the most powerful in any rich nation, the Genoa Social Forum proposed that local social forums be established, reflecting the diversity of the various anti-global groups, but reaching out more actively to the majority whom these movements believe they represent.

Writing the horror: intellectuals against global capitalism

Buttressing the emergence of the new movements was a new style of writing about the world – one that had links with older, Marxist versions of anti-capitalist polemic, but which was less theoretical, drawing more on personal experience and eyewitness accounts (though Marx and Engels were both good at that). The new authors felt no need to privilege the role of the industrial working class in a future revolution: unencumbered by the years of groupuscule wrangling, they preferred to be vague as to the processes they were describing. They tended to see them all as oppressive, where Marxists would divide them into those that the working class could use and those they would need to change or defeat. The surviving Marxists could sneer, but they could not beat them, and thus many joined them.

One can find 'anti-globalisation' or anti-American writing everywhere: in the brilliant, if introverted, writings of the ageing Russian dissident Alexander Solzhenitsyn and in the work of his much younger compatriots Julia Latynina and Victor Pelevin; in the nationalistic, 'anti-self-hating' literature of the Japanese patriotic circles, including the highly popular comics of Kobayashi Yoshinori; in the exhumation of Hindu myths to buttress the anti-multiculturalist nationalism of the BJP administration; in the heavily anti-Western and anti-Semitic messages that saturate newspapers, television and popular fiction in the Arab world. In the West, the most scathing (and bestselling) attacks on contemporary capitalism and media have come from France's intellectual left: for example, Pierre Bourdieu's *La*

Misere du Monde, Viviane Forrester's *L'Horreur Economique* or Serge Halimi's *Les Nouveaux Chiens de Garde*.

The dominant tone of anti-globalisation literature is harsh, the descriptions of the world nightmarish. The Anglo-American literature – among the most influential because of the dominance of the English language and the reach of Anglo-American radio and TV news – reflects this.

The new 'Anglo-Saxon writers' think of themselves as being in the belly of the capitalist beast. Though the harder edge of neoliberal Reaganism and Thatcherism has been softened, whether by their successors on the centre-right or by administrations of the centre-left, the new global writers see the policies as unchanged. Indeed, they regard these policies as worse because they are dressed in sheep's clothing.

Many of the economic-ideological pillars constructed in the 1980s that the global movements most despised remained in place in the 1990s. The economies of rich states increasingly conformed to the policies and reflexes hammered out in finance ministries and policy units in the 1980s: the imperatives were to keep the money tight and make the public private. Subsidies that kept coal mines open, state monopolies that kept competition away from publicly owned airlines, employment rules and practices that made dismissal difficult or impossible were abolished in radical versions such as Thatcherism, or were put under slow pressure in more gradualist versions such as successive Italian governments.

The route, whether taken by the hare or the tortoise, was seen as the same. The anti-globalisers came to see the adherence to this route as a kind of religion: the kind of religion that the Crusaders brought to the Muslim ('infidel') lands at the point of a sword. Susan George, a leading theorist of the anti-globalisation movement, wrote a book with Fabrizio Sabelli on the World Bank and called it pointedly *Faith and Credit*.[19] In a passage on the Bank's work in Africa, she quotes the Canadian scholar John Mihevc that 'the manner in which the World Bank has presented, promoted and defended structural adjustment against its critics closely parallels fundamentalist interpretations of the Bible. The strategies employed by the World Bank to guarantee the hegemony of its ideology and to deal with dissenters also correspond to those of fundamentalism.' George comments that, 'according to this theological interpretation, the Bank has contrived to confer on its own doctrines a status akin to that of divinely ordained natural law'. In a striking example of how someone largely concerned with global issues can also – in the global movements' network society – connect easily with the local, George turned up at the trial of Jose Bové in Millau, when he was arraigned for vandalising a McDonald's restaurant. 'It takes, she said, '43 seconds to make a McDonald's hamburger anywhere in the world. This uniformity is nothing less than a negation of peoples' culture.' It was the implicit expression of a new kind of justice, where the negation of culture by multinationals would finally be seen in just perspective against the minor damage done by a few up-against-the wall peasants to a multinational's latest attack on the people's right to retain their way of life.

In the 1990s, the first decade in which there was 'no coherent argument from any socialist left', there occurred a convergence of the views of commentators on the right and the left. The cold war, and the fact that socialism had 'coherent arguments', had kept them apart: now some began trading places. Those who were liberals as well as rightists began to think that the world in which they found themselves had reproduced some of the features of the worlds against which they had polemicised. Edward Luttwak, a man who 'deeply believes in the virtues of capitalism', nevertheless wrote in his 1998 book, *Turbo Capitalism*[20] (which he defined as societies remoulded to serve economies), that 'almost all western governments have had no better plan than to allow turbo-capitalism to advance without limit while hoping that faster growth will remedy all their shortcomings. That it will instead accelerate the fracturing of their societies into Silicon Valley heroes and vales of despond is suggested by all logic, but ignored by mainstream politics.'

The agreement between left and right was on the imperial pretensions of the new global capitalism: an imperial rule of capital whose coercion was – unlike previous empires – deeply hidden, but whose techniques of coercion were endlessly inventive and attractive. This – a cultural criticism turned activist and militant – is the core of Naomi Klein's work and success (especially in the UK, where her book *No Logo*[21] sold more than in any other market). Klein became the iconic author of the pack. She says *No Logo* is to show 'how, in ways both insidious and overt, [the] corporate obsession with brand identity is waging a war on public and individual space: on public institutions such as schools, on youthful identities, on the concept of nationality and on the possibilities for unmarketed space'. 'Waging war' is a strong phrase: it means that one side wishes to defeat, if not (as in much modern warfare) exterminate, the other.

It is a sign of the extreme disgust of this literary movement over the effects of capitalist globalisation that such language should be received without shock. It is clearly widely accepted that modern companies actually wish to destroy public institutions and private lives, invade and distort the experience of childhood and national identity, smash schools and bring everything under the dominance of the market. If this is no more than a routine description of corporate capitalism and of the states that support and promote it, no wonder it now meets such militant protest. Klein has distanced herself from the anti-globalisers who use violence, but her work insists on the question of whether violence, at least against the property of McDonald's, Starbucks, Nike, the World Bank or the WTO, has legitimacy where these corporations and institutions visit such repression on the globe. The conditions of real war that have taken shape in some parts of the world since 11 September may put the use of this language into a different perspective.

Klein's universe is one where corporations invade rich people's internal space, and do it by forcing poor people to work for them on subsistence wages. The corporate seducers are hip and cool, and see themselves as radical (I found this last description to be true when, in the process of interviewing a director of London's coolest ad agency, I was told that the agency had tried to persuade Klein to come over from Canada to talk to their staff). Corporate cool can go to extraordinary (verbal) extremes: for example, Klein quotes Tom Freston, CEO of the music station MTV (part of the giant Viacom corporation), as saying of MTV's president, Judy McGrath: 'Judy is inherently an anti-establishment person. Anyone who comes along and says – 'Let's off the pig' – has got her ear.'

Klein also quotes the marketing director of Starbucks, Scott Bradbury, as saying that the coffee-house chain wants to 'align ourselves with one of the greatest movements – towards finding a connection with your soul'. Madeleine Bunting, picking up Klein's theme, writes that 'consumer capitalism has appropriated the territory of purpose and meaning, refashioning them for its own ends ... the commercialisation of purpose and meaning as a means by which to sell products and services generates profound cynicism – the cynicism born of knowing and secretly despising our own susceptibility to the meanings we buy.'[22] Klein's talent has been to link the corporate soul merchants to the cheap-labour plants in the third world, making the people of the rich world feel that, by enjoying themselves, they are directly oppressing the poor. Her descriptions of workers in export processing zones in Manila are masterly journalism: '... it's obvious that the row of factories, each with its own gate and guard, has been carefully planned to squeeze the maximum amount of production out of this swathe of land. Windowless workshops made of cheap plastic and aluminium sidings are crammed in next to each other, only feet apart. Racks of time cards bake in the sun, making sure the maximum amount of time is extracted from each worker, the maximum amount of hours extracted from each day. The streets in the zone are eerily empty, and open doors – the ventilation system, for most factories – reveal lines of young women hunched in silence over clamouring machines.'

Corporations are seen to have substituted themselves for government. In *The Silent Takeover*[23], Noreena Hertz – who, like Luttwak, is not an anti-capitalist, distinguishes herself from the anti-globalisation radicals and says that 'capitalism is clearly the best system for generating wealth' – writes nevertheless that 'business has come to define the public realm', that taxes are being driven down by threats to move abroad, and that 'governments, by not even acknowledging the takeover, risk shattering the implicit contract between state and citizen that lies at the heart of a democratic society, making the rejection of the ballot box and support for non-traditional forms of political expression increasingly attractive'. The loss of faith in electoral politics – debate about which was greatly stimulated in the UK by a low turnout in the 2001 general election – is, according to this view, rational: the result of a recognition that one is voting for parties that no longer have more than a shell-like existence.

The theme of a world from which dissent – or, indeed, a point of view alternative to the dominant socio-economic paradigm – has been filtered out or marginalised is the most powerful in Thomas Frank's work, especially in *One Market Under God*[24], which is subtitled 'extreme capitalism, market populism and the end of economic democracy'. This book, like Klein's, is based on journalistic observation, and is similarly prone to slicing into these observations similes and predictions that conjure up horror beneath the pleasant, or the jokey, or the hip. Describing how an advertising campaign from the computer company Cisco Systems used children reading out 'testimonials to the internet', Frank writes: '[the children's] unsmiling faith in the goofy promises and even slightly threatening programmes of the "New Economy" puts one distinctly in mind of *1984*, with its noble child informers'. To compare a television ad for computers with the fictional totalitarianism of George Orwell's dystopia, itself based on the real Stalinist totalitarian state with its movement of youthful domestic espionage, is to read a nightmare into a jingle, and to conjure up a global prison from a packshot. It is another example of the extremely high verbal stakes routinely employed by the global movements' writers.

Frank (who sees Demos, the publisher of this pamphlet, as a collection of authors who 'round up various clichés from popular management literature and, adopting a tone of extreme historical righteousness, recast them as political advice') believes that Bill Clinton and Tony Blair 'took the lead in choking off dissent in the anglophone world'. Journalism has entered a 'time for the cessation of questioning'. The new management theories are either 'crackpot' or shamelessly self-serving. The issue of the language used by anti-globalisation activists deserves longer and separate study: it is enough here to note that it borrows a rhetoric of extremes from the Trotskyist left. Reflecting on the Asian-white riots in various UK cities in the summer of 2001, Ambalavaner Sivanandan, director of the Institute of Race Relations, wrote in *The Guardian*[25] that 'global capitalism, in its ruthless pursuit of markets and its sanctification of wealth, has served to unleash ethnic wars, balkanise countries and displace their peoples. The politics of exclusion is economic: a prelude to creating a peripatetic underclass of international *Untermenschen*.'

The grand global coalition: radicals united through networks

Anti-globalisation rhetoric and actions have deeply impressed some sections of the social democratic parties, particularly their left wings, as well as their left/Green partners in coalitions. In Italy, the Rifondazione Communista, a member of the Ulivo coalition that lost power in 2000, has become a major organising force for anti-gobalisation demonstrations, especially after the débâcle of Genoa. In France, the Communist Party and the Greens, both partners in the left coalition dominated by the Socialist Party, are active in the movement. In Germany, the Green Party, the Social Democrats' only coalition partner, has been riven by the pragmatic adjustments to power made by its leading member and the foreign minister, Joschka Fischer, who has a prominent history of far-left activism stretching from the 1960s to the 1980s. The party struggles desperately to hold on to its 'street' credentials as well as its state power.

In the UK, the Labour Party left is weaker, and tends to fight on more narrowly economist platforms than the left in Europe. But interest in the anti-globalisation struggle is growing: the MP Alan Simpson, secretary of the left-inclined Campaign Group of MPs, is foremost in proposing this perspective. In an article in *The Guardian*[26], he criticised Tony Blair and Chancellor Gordon Brown for their inclusion among the ranks of 'free trade fantasists', and wrote that the anti-globalisation struggle was being won 'by those who have decided they cannot go any further down the path of neoliberalism that corporations, the World Trade Organisation and compliant politicians would have us believe is the road to salvation'. The never-ending pressure of foreign competition on the labour markets of developed countries will continue to radicalise organised labour in Europe, as it has in the US, against globalisation. In autumn 2001, the trade union movement in Britain broadcast its sharpest warnings yet that it would not tolerate public sector privatisations that degrade the pay and conditions of its members – the sharp-end issue for all workers faced with a shift from relatively protected to relatively unprotected areas, and one that leftists such as Alan Simpson blame on globalisation. 'American corporations [are] queuing up for the guaranteed profit stream from privatised public services,' he writes, '... [yet] privatised markets in public services cost us more, deliver less, bequeath huge debts and generally walk off with the public's assets.'

In the second half of the 1990s, groups sprang up that sought not simply to counterpoise arguments on trade and investment and jobs, but physically to stop, or at least disrupt, the meetings of the institutions they deemed responsible for the state the world was in. They have grown up fast, and some have already disappeared, or have been merged into others. They are competitive with each other for members, money and exposure. Some have links with, and a few are fronts for, established Marxist, generally Trotskyist groups that did not go out of business in the 1990s; others are anarchist. Some – perhaps the most influential – have no ideological provenance, but have come into being to express an already settled conviction that governments, corporations and the global agencies are evil and must be stopped. A number of events are now seen as critical: Shell's secretive and insensitive handling of the Brent Spar oil rig collapse in the North Sea in 1995, and its apparent insouciance towards the effects of its oil exploitation in Nigeria's Ogoniland; BP's similar attitude to its workings in Colombia; Monsanto's trials with genetically modified soya beans. Shell's actions in Nigeria may, in retrospect, have been among the most important of these: they stimulated the opposition of Ken Saro-Wiwa, the playwright whose birthplace is Ogoniland, who was hanged by his government in 1995 – creating, as James Harding wrote in a *Financial Times* survey of the anti-globalisation movements, 'the first martyr of the counter-capitalist movement'.[27] Saro-Wiwa's dedication to his cause and his charismatic personality inspired a number of activists who met him, and who later started anti-globalisation organisations – such as Saoreen Amrose of '50 Years is Enough' (50 years, that is, of the IMF and World Bank), Steve Kretzman of Project Underground and John Sellers of the Ruckus Society.

In an extended interview in the *New Left Review*,[28] Sellers was revealing as to the attitudes and development of the new global movements. Before creating the Ruckus Society (which is defined on the back of activists' T-shirts as 'a loud angry interruption, a hullabaloo, a disruption), Sellers had worked for Greenpeace. A fellow activist called Mike Roselle, who had been a trainer in non-violent direct action, founded the society to stop deforestation in the US, basing it on Greenpeace's direct-action tactics. Sellers sees Ruckus as a link in a chain of actions and movements that use street protest, media coverage and the internet to 'build a truly global resistance to what is a completely global system of exploitation'. These groups are about 'strategically, non-violently raisin' hell because we don't like what's happening to the planet'. Sellers revealed that the tactics used in Seattle and since sprang from the kind of training camps that Greenpeace and other organisations used – with the direct action moving from rubber boats to the streets, and sharpened. The Direct Action Network, which played a large role in organising the Seattle demonstrations, was, he says, 'born at our camp two months before .. it was great to see all the different tools and gear that we granted out for the action being put to such good use by the people in the streets, the lock-down devices and well-trained people who put the blockade into place ... thirteen simultaneous actions made an incredible festival of resistance before the cops attacked and all hell broke loose. It was an amazing week, I'm very proud of our share in it.'

Sellers is clear that the movement encompasses 'classic Marxist, anti-capitalist energy', as well as people 'willing to take radical action to bring about a world with benign corporations, but they see the solution to our economic nightmare in something that would still look pretty much like it to people who want to get rid of the whole thing'. His own ideological compasses are Ghandi and Martin Luther King, both advocates of direct, non-violent mass action to shame the British, or the American whites, into support for independence and civil rights respectively. But the tactics have moved on. Speaking of an action against the US chain Home Depot, he says it was 'won not because it cut into corporate earnings, but because of a psychological campaign it waged against the CEO and board of directors. The message was: 'If you don't watch out, we're going to make you into the leper of every cocktail party that you go to – we're going to turn you into an oil executive!' '

For the non-violent Sellers, violence (at least against property) is not an absolute, but a relative matter: it depends how it is used, how it is seen. 'There is a big difference to me between Jose Bové and his French farmer friends and some of our anarchists here. They dismantled a McDonald's with their tractors while the whole town, including kids, had a picnic and a band played, with the community out in force to support this largely symbolic action. To a corporation like McDonald's, that's nothing – it was less than a drop in the bucket. There's a big difference between an action like that and four or five people in black masks celebrating a positive, forward-looking movement and smashing a few windows at McDonald's. Here you can really speak of a violent act, which may harm others and let the cops label us as "terrorists".' Later, Sellers says that, while on the Greenpeace ship Rainbow Warrior in the Mediterranean, he cut a French fisherman's driftnet that was an illegal length. 'The net belonged to a fisherman, but the global public knew why I was doing it.' These last comments are particularly rich in meaning. The Bové protest actually did more damage than the anarchists' rocks: the distinction Sellers makes is one between a mass, popular protest and one that hits and runs without any explanation or attempt to gain public sympathy. The 'global public' must be engaged; they must come to accept groups like Ruckus as the true guardians of the earth and its resources, as against the exploitative corporations and their guardians, the national governments and the international agencies. The activists assume the right to know that the 'global public' understands.

This echoes justifications for civil disobedience that can be found in liberal theory (such as Rawls), and assumes that the action is taken with a readiness to accept the legal punishment, and that the legal process itself will be used as an opportunity to put the motivations and arguments to a wider public – a tactic seen in the McDonald's libel trial. One difference is that the activists are appealing to the public on a global level; another is that their violence – even if the destruction is a 'drop in the bucket' to large corporations – tends to be both emulated and exceeded, while the readiness to accept legal punishment is evident only where the trials can be turned into public theatres.

Although the US groups are frequently the most self-assured, best funded and most visible, the French group Attac is among the most influential. Begun in 1999 by Bernard Cassen (see above) of *Le Monde Diplomatique* in combination with a number of Latin American radicals, Attac's main formal agenda is to press for the adoption of the Tobin Tax. Named after its inventor, James Tobin, now Sterling

Professor Emeritus of Economics at Yale University, this would be a transaction tax – a mere 0.05 per cent – on money transfers. The idea, as Tobin described it in the 1971 Janeway Lecture at Princeton, was to dampen speculation and arbitrage by raising the price on repeated transactions and thus rewarding those who do 'fundamental' business requiring few transfers. It would also, he believed, preserve some measure of national financial autonomy by giving the national central banks some leeway to adjust short-term interest rates. The proceeds were not of much interest to him: he thought they might go to finance the activities of the World Bank, of which he was, and is, a strong supporter. Ideally, he wanted these proceeds to diminish to very little, because he wanted many fewer transactions. 'But,' he wrote in the *Financial Times*[29], 'revenue may be the Tobin Tax's principal attraction for its enthusiasts, along with the mistaken notion that it would be a blow against the alleged evils of globalisation.'

But the radicals of *Le Monde Diplomatique* – perhaps the most influential paper of the left in the world, with a very large circulation in a number of languages – were not interested in what the inventor thought: they had discovered a mobilisation point for global idealism. In Attac, they had found a vehicle for a network that spread rapidly across Europe, attracting people for whom the Tobin Tax was but one weapon in a whole armoury to pit against the evils of globalisation. Attac, like *Le Monde Diplomatique*, is uncompromisingly anti-American, scornful of its own and other European governments (especially that of the UK) and committed to a neo-Marxist reading of world developments, enriched by the continued radicalism of that section of the French intelligentsia who did not move to the centre or the right in the 1980s.

The sweet smell of excess: the impact of the new movements

The success of the global movements can scarcely be overemphasised. In roughly five years, they have grown from a collection of disparate groups with quite separate strategies and programmes to a movement linked together in opposition to something called globalisation. Many protest, rightly, that they are not opposed to globalisation, only to capitalist globalisation, or aspects of globalisation: that is why they are referred to here as 'global' rather than 'anti-globalisation' movements.

But there is no doubt that the impact they have made on the public mind is of opposition to contemporary globalisation and to the governments and institutions that support it. Their success is such that a small group of local residents objecting to a motorway bypass can feel part of a movement linking them to campaigns to save the rainforests or protests against damage to the ozone layer.

Only in the global movements, it seems, does there survive, in some form, the sense of a popular current driving to transform the world by ridding it of a system that ruins and oppresses. Only there do the socialist themes – of public/popular/state as superior to private/capitalist ownership; of equality of reward; of the overthrow of imperialism; of the tyranny of corporate power over individual lives; of the impoverishment of the wretched; of the mendacity of the capitalist/official media – find expression, in slogans, campaigns and rhetoric. Socialism – real socialism – has migrated from the national to the global: it finds comradeship on the internet; it comes together in mega-demonstrations in the cities that capital's guardians choose for their conventions – Seattle, Washington, Prague, Gothenburg or Genoa.

At these events, projects and prominent figures are now routinely subjected to mass, at times violent, protest in the name of a higher – and at least partly socialist – morality. The movements have capitalised on the shards and splinters of socialist themes lying semi-abandoned after the great collapse of the late 1980s and early 1990s, have infused them with new life and reorganised them along new trajectories. Very rapidly – the speed perhaps reflecting the avidity with which the media swallow, chew over and regurgitate anything with the label 'new' attached – these themes have become part of the mindset of the educated, especially the young educated, of most wealthy and middle-income countries.

They weave in and out of patterns of media choice, consumerism and lifestyles both as adjuncts to and critiques of the lives lived. They attract at least a guilty twitch of assent from all but the most dedicated pro-capitalists – including many who would regard themselves as rightist, who correctly see in the various forces of globalisation threats to the institutions and patterns of life that sustained and expressed their beliefs and patterns of living. The media savvy of the new movements has thrown up a range of attitudes that many modern liberal/leftists, especially if young, feel ought to be respected: such as disapproving of McDonald's and Starbucks, eschewing conspicuous consumption, and scorning mass American culture.

These movements are currently at a high water mark. They have pushed back the corporations, governments and agencies that evacuate sectors which prove too embarrassing, or change their strategies to accommodate their critics, or seek dialogue with them. In many ways, those whom Sellers describes as wishing for a 'world of benign corporations' are achieving at least some of their ends. But for most of the anti-globalisers, the world remains much as it was – and the governing centre-left is defending it. What can that left – and a broader left – do about that? Is this the latest version of the old 20th-century cleavage between reformers and revolutionaries – a globalised form of what, since the passing of the Comintern, had been a largely national phenomenon?

4. The challenge to social democracy

The global challenge to the social democratic or centre-left is clear. It is to articulate a response to the charge that the institutions of politics and governance, including economic and developmental governance, are systematically failing to account for or respect the basic needs of most of the world's population. As a result, the charge goes, politics is failing, and those politicians of the left with a special claim to be concerned about inequality and disadvantage are at best hypocrites, at worst puppets of corporate and financial interests. The accusation comes from groups that have strong bases in most developed countries, as well as global links. These groups are sophisticated and inventive in their use of technology (especially the internet) and in their protest tactics; they have access to substantial funds from their supporters and a group of rich well-wishers; and they cover a wide spectrum, from groups whose main purpose is to cause violence and provoke counter-violence through to well-established NGOs, whose origins lie in religious or ethical impulses, and whose practice is so well accepted that they are used as agents for government programmes.

These groups are increasingly divided on strategies of protest. But they unite in proposing much tighter curbs on the effects, or presumed effects, of globalisation than the governments of most states, both rich and poor, have been willing to accept. They appeal to young people, offer outlets for energy, idealism and indignation, and have a cause, or multiple causes, in which people can believe, and which can give the believers a sense that they are better people for holding the beliefs they do.

Above all, they are network organisations, confronting governments and organisations that are still largely trapped in hierarchical models. Governments remain in these models partly because they carry different and much more onerous responsibilities, which can be fulfilled only through identifiable chains of command. But to an extent this trap is of their own making, through inertia and lack of an impulse to modernise. Yet when they do become more oriented to service delivery, they necessarily diminish their inspirational role.

The new movements fulfill that inspirational role above all others. They answer many social and emotional demands that have historically been placed on political parties of the left. And they do so at a time when the surge of support for the centre-left that was such a feature of the second half of the 1990s is no longer rising. All leftist parties – in common with almost all parties – are suffering an erosion of membership, particularly among the young, who vote in much smaller numbers than their parents' generation, and join or stay in parties far more rarely.

The centre-left surge of the late 1990s is checked, and receding. The Democrats lost the White House. The Bush administration is ideologically further right than the candidates' proclamation of 'compassionate conservatism' and his own moderate record as governor of Texas led many to believe. The Italian Ulivo left coalition lost power to a revived right that has a substantial far-right component. The Spanish left, which had governed through lean times for the European left in the 1980s, lost power in the 1990s and failed to win it back in 2000. In September 2001, the ruling Norwegian Labour Party received its biggest electoral humbling since the 1920s: its share of the vote was reduced to less than 25 per cent of the electorate, after receiving 35 per cent four years before. Most of the gains went to the Conservatives, on the neoliberal right, which campaigned on lower taxes and better education (this in a country with some of the highest living standards in the world, enjoying decades of large oil revenues). The French Socialists, who also claim only around 25 per cent of the electorate, are making no gains in the polls ahead of a presidential election year. And Germany's ruling Social Democrats are slipping from the high rating that Chancellor Gerhard Schroeder had enjoyed, in part, because of the financial scandals that rocked the Christian Democrats.

These setbacks have occurred in countries with high growth

(Norway) and low growth (Italy), for both governments that have been concerned to maintain a more leftist image (France) and those that have publicly trumpeted a more centrist policy (Germany). As of autumn 2001, only the British Labour Party has bucked that trend, with poll ratings still well above 40 per cent. It still easily beats a Conservative Party that imploded after the 2001 election defeat, while the third-placed Liberal Democrats are not yet able to replace the Conservatives as the main opposition party.

None of the social democratic parties has been able to avoid the by-products of office: compromise, responsibility and the expression of a national interest that they can define only to a limited degree. Governments inherit a network of obligations, secrets, tacit under-standings and alliances that time, expedience and necessity oblige them to keep. Inevitably, they suffer from scandals. The measures they take to save or increase jobs, to augment public provision, to spread the benefits of education more widely and improve its quality, to improve public health provision, to combat racism and other exclu-sions, to strengthen trade unions, to improve international co-opera-tion, to inject an ethical dimension into foreign policies – and all left-of-centre governments recently or now in power did or are doing all of these – are discounted or seen as meagre. When they seek directly to address the global movements' agenda – for instance, when, in autumn 2001, the French prime minister endorsed the Tobin Tax and the German chancellor added conditional support; or when the UK government played a leading part in cancelling a substantial propor-tion of third world debt – it is ignored by many anti-globalisation groups, or dismissed as public relations.

Above all, none of the centre-left parties can easily live with the loss of coherent socialism. Coherent socialism offered them all an aim: one that was never attained, but against whose scale some successes could be notched up. It gave the parties campaigning and recruiting themes; it kept the loyalty of the industrial working class (rarely a majority, but for many years of the 20th century the most numerous socio-economic group); it offered a public service ethic that could leak into the private sector. Now it cannot be articulated as it was. There is no longer a series of pinnacles to be conquered – such as the nation-alisation of leading enterprises, or the replacement of capitalist with socialist relations in the workplace, or the provision of more and more public services for free.

In these and other areas, the reverse is usually true: privatisation continues in all states governed by the centre-left; the dominant workplace practices are those given by the new management wisdom that stresses flexibility, independence and profit-centred work; and more and more public services are being taken into the private sector, or are being charged for. The rhetoric has thus moved to values. That pleases the anti-globalisation groups, because it is at least as easy to show that values are being flouted as it was for the Marxist groups to show that social democrats were reneging on their economic programmes. The centre-left must watch from its offices of power as the idealism that is still embroidered on its banners, that is still (sometimes) proclaimed in its rhetoric and still animates the hearts and minds of its most active members – including its leading politicians – is captured and/or mocked on the streets.

The loss of socialism created an impulse towards modesty and pragmatism as to what government action could achieve, which has made the contrast with the global movements even sharper. Those governments that have dedicated themselves to creating a stability (social order, low inflation) within which they can pursue limited progressive objectives, such as high public service investment, incremental income redistribution and urban regeneration, are finding that they do not have a central political narrative strong enough to convince electorates of their progressive credentials. Perhaps even worse, they are finding that the stable framework they hoped to create and occupy is being directly challenged and pulled apart by the critique and the protest actions of the new movements.

The centre-left will sooner or later have to face and answer the central question posed by the anti-globalisation movements: how is the globe to be managed? What are the structures and systems, the forums and movements, that can articulate the ideals and aims of social democracy in a world whose global actors are disturbingly over-represented by capital, finance and media – or even by crime groups – and which lacks a powerful democratic counterweight? The issues and tactics thrown up by the new movements demand a response that is careful in two ways: careful to recognise the depth of the problems and miseries they flag up, and how much their alleviation is an integral part of the left's concern; and careful to distinguish these issues from strategies and tactics that harm solution by preferring confrontation, or that prefer dogma to examination.

The five challenges:
Violence

The violent tactics of some of the demonstrators have attracted a huge amount of media attention. The established groups protest against this, arguing that the bulk of demonstrators are non-violent, and often actively deplore the use of violence. In this, they are partly right: violence against property and the police is the tactic of, typically, a few hundred in a demonstration of thousands. Because their actions are inherently dramatic, they attract the camera, the microphone and the photographer's lens. Activist violence in this context, and its privileging by the media, did not arise first in Seattle: it flared up in Birmingham during the G8 summit, when 'in the evening, instead of going home, about a hundred vandals marched towards the city centre with the objective of breaking windows. The next day's papers, in the main, gave an account almost wholly dedicated to these people.'[30]

But the problem has another side. The global movements of the 1970s and 1980s used the media bias towards drama as a major player in their own growth and success. Media organisations entered into active partnership with NGOs to show misery, famine and war. They went with activists who tried to stop whaling or oil exploration. Often, the actions were taken in order to create images for the media. A strategy that depends on the media's predilection for action is caught on the back foot when some activists cross a line between protest and violence.

For social democrats in governments, simply relying on strengthened policing or shifting future conference venues to inaccessible resorts is not enough. For global movements opposed to violence, a disavowal of their violent colleagues is also not enough. There must be an explicit engagement in encouraging and developing the anti-violence codes that a number of groups – such as Friends of the Earth – have proposed, and these should be signed and adhered to by all groups participating in protest actions.

An approach sketched out by Daniel Cohn-Bendit, a leading member of the German Green Party, is one to be explored. In an interview in *Le Monde*,[31] Cohn-Bendit argued for 'a democratic situation where a strategy of violence has no reason to exist. I think we should establish a kind of demilitarised zone around the conference centres where summits take place. I suggest that no police should be deployed in that zone, but that 2,000 citizens, MPs, members of political parties or organisations which wish to protect peacefully, by their presence, the conference building [to protect it] from the intrusion of certain activists. The leaders of the anti-globalisation movement must understand that a permanent strategy of developing violence will cause the movement to disintegrate.'

Cohn-Bendit's unequivocal distaste for extremes is a much better approach than the blame-the-other-side responses of Klein and Sellers (even though both of these express opposition to violence). It is also likely to be more fruitful than shifting conference venues to distant and impregnable locations, as was proposed by many after the débâcle of the G8 summit in Genoa in July 2001. Violence of the kind seen on demonstrations tends to play into the hands of those who favour tough action, because it provides a basis of public support for such action. More to the longer-term point, it devalues, by association, the arguments of those who are worth listening to.

Governments committed to upholding and extending civil rights must protect the civil right to protest. They are entitled to ask for civility from protesters. They must take the lead in establishing game rules for international gatherings that are likely to be the focus of protest. These must rule out violence, but must also ensure that the gatherings can take place without concerted efforts to close the venue or blockade the town.

The debates within the forums that many protesters wish to close down are often about alleviating the ills that the global movements make their cause. To close them down merely shifts discussion to other gatherings – usually national governments – thus devaluing the transnational institutions that have the potential to represent the interests of all nations, not merely the powerful. The paradox of the protests is that they tend to damage the forums that, although flawed, give the poorest some voice. This is increasingly – if often reluctantly – realised on the part of the mass global movements, and this assists governments in developing a response. Though dramatic, it is among the easiest of the challenges.

Anti-Americanism

In *The Lexus and the Olive Tree*[32], Thomas Friedman likens the US to a gas station in which the gas is cheap but the customer must serve himself – contrasting that with other parts of the world, where either the gas is expensive but served to you, or cheap but unavailable because it has been sold on the black market. 'What is going on,' he writes, 'is that through the process of globalisation everyone is being forced towards America's gas station. If you are not American and don't know how to pump your own gas, I suggest you learn . . . in so many ways, globalisation is us. We are not the tiger. Globalisation is the tiger. But we are the people most adept at riding the tiger and now we're telling everyone else to get on or get out of the way.'

Friedman's book was in part an explanation of why globalisation and America are seen as one and disliked. In his travels around the world for the *New York Times*, Friedman would constantly discover anti-Americanism. In Tehran, the slogan 'Down with the USA' is tiled into the wall of a hotel: outside, Iranian mullahs call the US 'the capital of global arrogance'. He does an interview with a 'man in the street' in Baghdad, and is told that America is 'an international Dracula that sucks the blood of the people around the world'. The Indian finance minister tells him, more politely, that 'there is no balance, no counterpoise: whatever you say is law.' A former Algerian prime minister at a conference in Morocco, tells Friedman that 'this globalisation you speak about is just another American conspiracy to keep the Arab world down, just like imperialism and Zionism'. A letter to a Japanese (English language) newspaper reads: 'the world's 'greatest country' must learn humility. Pride comes before a fall. The US government would do well to remember that.'

The terrorists' attempt to engineer that fall from pride was demonstrated on 11 September 2001. Those who shake their fist at America have seen their hatred realised in ways in that – presumably – most did not want. The terrorism displayed in New York and Washington was often fantasised, but there is little evidence that most who proclaimed anti-Americanism actually wanted the deaths of thousands of

Americans. The global movements are not terrorists – no matter how aggressive their tactics have been. But terrorism draws moral support from a general climate, one in which the US is identified as some sort of an oppressor.

Radical Islamic groups are in a class of their own when it comes to hating America. In different areas in different ways, they have developed a shifting narrative of victimisation at the hands of the West in general and America in particular. The war against Iraq and the continuing sanctions on that country; the attacks launched on Libya with the intent to kill Colonel Gaddafi; the sanctions, applied particularly by the US, on Iran; US support for Israel, seen as an occupier of Muslim land and a bridgehead of imperialism – these are part of a litany of justification for hatred, and provide a sea of acceptance for the 11 September action. Osama Bin Laden, the Saudi multimillionaire turned *mujahid* who is suspected of organising the terrorist action, has made clear in successive interviews his loathing for America, and has sought to give it the status of a jihad, or religious war. 'Hostility towards America is a religious duty, and we hope to be rewarded for it by God,' he said in an interview with *Time* in 1999. He has identified Jews and 'Crusaders' (Christians) as imperialists on Muslim soil, to whom the fight must be carried. He represents the sharpest and most extreme edge of a loose movement of groups and states that have identified imperialism, materialism, godlessness and immorality – all reaching their acme in America – as objects of active hostility, as enemies in a fitful but real war. Bin Laden is also, in part, a product of the last days of the anti-Soviet campaigns: trained and armed with thousands of others by the CIA, he gained his self-confidence through fighting the Soviet army in Afghanistan in the 1980s – learning there that, once the Soviet Union was destroyed, America must be next.

The Middle Eastern states have for long tended to see the US – at least publicly – through their hostility to Israel. In the 1990s, the traditional distaste for the US as Israel's protector was fleshed out with a fiercer hatred, which saw the West in general as an oppressor. Even where, as in the Gulf war, Muslim states expressed hostility to Saddam Hussein and support for the US-led intervention and war against Iraqi forces, they were usually forced by public pressure to backtrack on their support before the war's end. In turn, the US tends to see the Islamic fundamentalism professed by some governments and movements in the region – especially Iran in the 1980s and early 1990s – as a new ideological threat to the West. President George Bush talked of Saddam Hussein as 'Hitler revisited'; the conservative commentator Charles Krauthammer described Iran as 'the world's new Comintern'. The 1998 bombing of the World Trade Center in New York by Islamic extremists associated with Bin Laden – which was intended to kill many more than it did and to topple the twin towers – brought home for the first time the sense that a religious civilisation had dedicated itself to America's humbling.

In *The Clash of Civilisations* – a work that grew sharply in influence after 11 September – Samuel Huntington shows that Muslim states were involved in far more 'intergroup violence' at the end of the 20th century than other civilisations. He suggests a range of explanations: that Islam has been, from its inception, a 'religion of the sword', and Mohammed a noted military commander; that the religion spread quickly and widely, and (as with any empire) it left behind many conflicts; that Muslim societies are 'indigestible', in that they are militant in their faith and communal values, whether as a majority or a minority within states; that the surge of Western power in the past two centuries left a general sense of inferiority and resentment, and an impression of weakness that allows Muslims to be victimised; that, in the past two or three decades, there has been a birth explosion in Muslim societies, producing very many, often unemployed, young men; and finally, that Islam has no one centre, and thus there is fierce competition between states and groups for one to prove itself the leader – often by being militantly anti-American.

There are accounts of Islam that cut against Huntington's. Karen Armstrong sees the rapid race for modernisation in Muslim states as a large reason for their militancy, as they seek to undertake in decades what Western states did in centuries – centuries of horrendous wars. Amartya Sen[33] insists that 'the presence of diversity and variety within [Islamic] tradition' is as strong as in Christian traditions: he cites the case of Akbar, the late 16th-century Mogul emperor, who issued an edict from Delhi in 1591 to the effect that 'no man should be interfered with on account of his religion, and anyone is to be allowed to go over to any religion he pleased'. Sen adds that 'while Akbar was making these pronouncements, the Inquisitions were in full bloom in Europe'. The 20th-century history of Indonesia, the world's largest Muslim state, shows – especially in the later decades – an ebb and flow in the power of liberal and radical Muslims. The latter, however, tended to win out as the century ended.

Whatever history may show, and whatever has produced the phenomenon, the current radical Muslim hostility is unmatched by other states or groups – including Russia and China. At the same time, because the largest reserves of oil are in Arab-Muslim hands, the West has made strenuous efforts to support the ruling dynasties in the 'pro-Western' states, especially Saudi Arabia. On the agenda of the radical Muslim groups is the replacement of these dynasties, seen as corrupt and insufficiently Islamic, with their own rulers – a nightmare for the West.

The West has, over the past few decades, developed a series of attitudes and passed a raft of laws outlawing discrimination on racial or religious grounds. Western countries, particularly the US, have taken in hundreds of thousands of immigrants from Asian states – including Afghans fleeing from the Taliban regime with whom Bin Laden is allied. Their rights to separate religious practices are guaranteed. America has been a pioneer of multiculturalism – a policy often contentious, but never seriously challenged. The US and EU states have made it a plank of their foreign and aid policies, recommending multicultural solutions to states whose ethnic groups live in hostility to each other – as they did in the states of former Yugoslavia into which they were drawn by war. The West has put pressure on states throughout the former communist bloc to treat as full citizens those ethnic minorities whom they were prone to regard as potential traitors or troublemakers, or second-class citizens. The extension of full civil rights to these minorities has been held up as a necessary condition for the receipt of aid, and for future membership of Nato and the EU. The success of these strategies has varied, but they have been seriously pursued.

At the moment, it appears that a significant strain within Islam – certainly present in groups that claim to be the religion's most fervent disciples – now regard Western values and customs, and often

Westerners themselves, as intolerable. The rejection of Western culture at times makes no distinction between a distaste for American TV and films (one shared by most European cultural elites) and a contempt for attitudes and strategies, say, to end discrimination against women or homosexuals. An effort to be inclusive meets a rejection of the very philosophy of a multicultural society – including by those living within multicultural societies.

These elements within Muslim societies represent a large and continuing problem between these societies and the West, one that the events of 11 September have thrown into harsh relief. They are particularly severe for social democrats, because the values of the centre-left have been to the fore in adumbrating practices and legislation against discrimination and for the extension of civil and human rights. It was a conservative figure, the Italian premier Silvio Berlusconi, who in September 2001 bluntly stated in a speech in Berlin that Western civilisation was 'superior' to the Islamic one because of the former's development of civil rights. It was a bad time to say it, when a broad coalition, including many Islamic states, was being constructed against terrorism; and it proposed a hierarchy of civilisations that flies against the necessary respect shown to other cultures. But it forced, or should have forced, the left to reflect that its strategies for the betterment of mankind are often seen as intolerable and imperialistic intrusions into other states' and societies' networks of customs, traditions and laws.

The global movements' anti-Americanism must be distinguished from that of radical Islam. It is not religious; it has a brief history (though it borrows from the history of the revolutionary left); it does not depend on territory or the control of resources. Though some of the websites used by the more radical global groups produced anti-American outbursts after 11 September, these did not appear to reflect a major strand of opinion. Most global groups called off demonstrations planned to take place in the immediate aftermath of the attacks, and made clear their opposition to terrorism.

Yet the anti-Americanism that develops into, or at least supports, terrorism presents a challenge to the anti-Americanism of some of the global movements. It plays on some of the same strings; and given that it is now so obvious that the stakes are very high, those who hold these views must make a careful accounting of how seriously they do so. The intellectually lazy anti-Americanism, which is a lingua franca of these movements, tends to use the US as a proxy for global threat.

This is as destructive of efforts to create and build effective global institutions as is a unilateralist stance by the current US administration. An insistence that the US is the sole or largest element of any global problem leads to revulsion on the part of the majority of the US population. It also confirms the belief of some developing countries that they have no need of internal reform, a state of mind fatally easy to develop. Many Russians, for example, including those in positions of power, took refuge in the view that lack of reform in the post-Soviet period was a consequence of Western, largely US, mistakes and lack of support (or too much support). This view was fleshed out with a belief that Western aid and advice was aimed at making Russia, and all of the former Soviet states, dependent on the West for ever, and always submissive.

The only political grouping now using the tactics developed by the global movements – sporadic use of violence and oppositionism through uncontrollable and unpredictable networks – is Bin Laden's al-Qaeda. In taking the destructive potential of such tactics and strategies to a far more lethal extreme, they have shown that the line of attack developed by the global movements cannot replace the current system of world governance. A different approach, though it is likely to build network organisational forms and political coalitions in non-traditional ways, is needed to create real progressive change and develop positive responses to the problems faced by three-quarters of the world's population.

Reasoned argument can make a case that undifferentiated hostility destroys. If, for example, an argument is to be mounted against the sanctions being applied by the West, led by the US, on Iraq, that argument will win little respect if it ignores the human rights violations practised by the Iraqi leadership within its national borders, as well as the threat Iraq poses to surrounding states by its development of weapons of mass destruction. Or any opposition to America's deployment of National Missile Defence and the scrapping of the 1972 Anti-Ballistic Missile Treaty has to recognise the threat to America – which to most will now seem more real – from a rocket-carried nuclear bomb, the substantial redundancy of the 1972 agreement and the much wider availability of nuclear technology to small states and to terrorist groups since the collapse of the Soviet Union. An opposition that is just denunciation will succeed only in hardening positions. The global movements have many good arguments against policies and programmes of the US administration, which identify threats to the construction of a safer, cleaner and more just world. Some are careful to make a discrimination between these and general hostility to the US. Others do not, and in that lack of discrimination lie the seeds of a moral ambiguity over the justification for acts taken against it or its interests.

European governments, whose Union constitutes the only alternative pole of Western global influence, have now a particular responsibility to use their influence to draw the US into creating the institutions of an interdependent world. These institutions – those created at Bretton Woods, those developed or developing since, such as the EU, and those in embryo – must now take over more and more of the burden of global governance from states, including states as powerful as the US. They must develop sufficient common strength and influence to demonstrate that a world of supranational institutions is a more secure and rewarding one than a flight into defiant strength. That is both harder and much more urgent after Manhattan. It is particularly the task of social democratic governments – which must have the conviction of their ideals to argue the case with the present US administration.

There is no question that the US administration, and more deeply the mood it represents, presents a large challenge to centre-left-led European governments. They could ignore it during Bill Clinton's presidency, because he sought to share many of the concerns and values of European left governments. Now, however, US and European policies are in more evident conflict, and lie deep under the solidarity shown in the face of the Manhattan and Pentagon attacks. US unilateralism; its recoil from efforts – such as the proposed international criminal court – to establish norms of international justice; its unwillingness, until after 11 September, to restrain the Israeli government's destruction (in awful symmetry with the Palestinian leadership) of a base for future negotiations; its determination to put domestic growth above any considerations of ecological damage to the biosphere; its unequivocal commitment to a defence system that compromises all other defence strategies – all of these directly or largely contradict the tentative efforts made by European states to globalise justice, equity and representation as well as business and media. If, as Robert Cooper writes[34], 'solving the problem of international legitimacy will be the major challenge for the 21st century', it is a challenge to which the US has not seemed willing to rise.

The terrorist attacks on America may lead to a change in this attitude. In the immediate aftermath, pressure was put on the Israeli government to hold talks with the Palestinian leadership, and the most aggressive strategy options to revenge the attacks appear to have been discarded. Allies of the US must continue both to support it and to influence it towards recognising the world's interdependence, in which it is the largest single element. In the early stages of the action against Aghanistan, the US actively considered how a post-military strategy should develop, and how institutions such as the UN could be involved in any recovery strategy and peacekeeping. On an optimistic assessment made by some on the left, the US has been shocked out of its unilateralism. This is unlikely to be wholly true, but the need to rethink polices following 11 September may provide a basis for a different approach.

Americans who have encountered, since 11 September, anti-Americanism in other rich countries such as the UK have been shocked by it: in their view, the US has been a generous and patient exporter of democracy, popular culture and foreign aid. That view is not complete, but it is not wrong. As it was put in the *Economist*[35]: 'a foreign policy designed to widen the reach of democracy is not an imposition of Western ideas' (though it may be seen as such, as I have discussed). It is cruel folly to argue that the US 'had it coming' because of real or alleged actions over the past decade or more. US policy has become much less covertly subversive of states seen as enemies and more accommodating of differences; where it has opposed others, it has done so openly, and on internationally defensible grounds – for example, in repelling the Iraqi invasion of Kuwait in 1991, and in pushing back the Serbs from Kosovo in 1998 (in both cases, acting in defence of a Muslim state or region). If the US has done too little to restrain Israel and has been too much in thrall to the power of the

Jewish lobby at home, it has not – until this year – renounced obligations to assist the search for peace in the Middle East, a search supported by the Palestinian and other Arab leaderships.

As superpowers go, at least historically, US rule is relatively benign. But it has not yet succeeded – and before 11 September it was not seriously attempting to succeed – in even sketching out a global institutional architecture in which all could find a place. Yet this is the best route to bolster its security. The export of democracy is a legitimate project, but democracy cannot be imposed by military force, because that negates the value of its export. We should recognise that some kinds of economic assistance have been experienced by recipients as a different form of coercion; and democracy levered in as a quid pro quo for aid often ends up being formal only. Yet to come is a debate that contrasts different models of democracy and civil society around the world in order to learn from them, as we currently do with industrial structures or national cultures of capitalism. Such a debate cannot take place without the recognition that variations from the standard western model can take place. The opportunity for different societies is to develop their own models as part of an evolutionary approach to modernisation and democratisation.

Anti-capitalism

Anti-capitalism has been the major theme of socialism, in all its forms, for more than a century. For those on the socialist left everywhere, it remains so – now refreshed with the themes of the global movements, to which leftists have greatly contributed. The centre-left has made a more explicit accommodation of capitalism than at any time in socialism's history – none more explicit than New Labour. But the subject remains an exposed nerve. Most members of leftist parties, including ministers and other senior officials, have their intellectual and ideological (as well as emotional) roots in a recent past in which a commitment to socialism was part of the party furniture. They cleave to variants of the 'traditional values in a modern setting' phrase used by new Labour to reassure members and supporters that the ends have not changed, even if the means have. But they remain sensitive to charges of deserting the commanding heights of socialist policy and action, and the global movements make full use of this.

These movements are largely anti-capitalist. Although, as John Sellers said (p 51), they incorporate groups and individuals who are reformist and, as noted, the right finds many common causes with them, the dominant strain of the past few years has been a harsh critique of capitalism and an at least implicit sense that it should be replaced by a better system. The critique is not rigorous: it tends to blur into convenient (to the movement) vagueness on how far it is for reform, or how far it is for abolition. But the main movement is unmistakable. The opposition to the policies of the international financial institutions is because they assist business; the opposition to governments is that they are subordinate to business; the opposition to business is that it destroys the planet, democracy and human lives. The deeper source from which the global movements gain force and moral vigour is from being directed against what Luttwak calls 'turbo-capitalism'. The spread of capitalism around the world has produced, almost everywhere, a global overclass, defined not just by wealth, but by technocratic skills. Countering that is a majority, everywhere outside of the rich countries, who do not or cannot share in that wealth, and whose resentments turn not just against their own elites, but against the rulers of an unfair world. This insight is not confined to radicals. In his latest book, Henry Kissinger (notably more mordant about the effects of globalisation than Thomas Friedman) reflects on the emergence of a 'two-tiered system [in which] globalised elites – often living in fortified suburbs – are linked by shared values and technologies, while the populations at large in the cities are tempted by nationalism, ethnicity and a variety of movements to free themselves from what they perceive to be the hegemony of globalisation, frequently identified with American domination . . . in such an environment, globalisation could easily evolve into a new ideological radicalism.'

The centre-left is committed to the successful workings of capitalism. It is also too embedded in the philosophy and practice of reformist politics to allow itself to be manoeuvred out of strategies for improving the market's workings, and developing or creating the means and will to do so.

Corporations, depicted by the anti-globalisation movement as monoliths, are now more fragile than they were for much of the post-war

20th century. They have always existed through the will of states, whose legislatures extend them the right to corporate existence. They are now more vulnerable to changes in demand and fashion, and to competition from various parts of the globe, than they were in more stable – that is, more cartelised and protected – times. When times are hard, corporations are much more fragile than states. While the largest among them have reserves that allow them to survive setbacks, a bad run is more likely to finish them in a 21st-century hyper-competitive environment than it was in the 20th century.

They have, on the other hand, largely taken the upper hand over organised labour. In all advanced economies in the decades after the war, the labour movement strengthened for both economic and political reasons. Enterprises grew in size and workers were thus structurally encouraged to see their interests as common and best advanced by joint action. The public sector grew hugely, and often welcomed unionisation, or put no barriers in its way. An influential strain of management thinking called for consensual management of workplaces, in which strong unions were thought essential to provide an authoritative bargaining partner. The success of social democratic parties was crucially dependent on financial and popular support from unions and union members; thus the unions' interests were advanced by social democrats in government, while the governing parties of the right did not usually seek substantially to roll back union gains. Where an administration tried, as the 1960-64 Heath government did in the UK, it suffered both industrial and political punishment.

Much of that changed in the 1980s and 1990s, and the change was only partly due to the confrontational stance of governments such as Margaret Thatcher's and Ronald Reagan's. More important were the structural changes: the reduction of workforces, the growth of small businesses, the huge expansion of the service sector and the contraction of public sector employment. Privatisation, a major element of Thatcherism and of its perceived success around the world, was politically driven: it has, however, been copied and furthered by leftist administrations, and is generally seen by governments as an answer to an overstretched state and public sector sluggishness.

The relative 'freedom' from the pressures of organised labour, however, has been accompanied not just by the greater competitive pressures of an increasingly globalised market place, but also by the high-profile opposition of activist groups – who often speak for and in the name of poor workers in developing states. The opposition is expressed both in general terms and to particular cases: such as oil company operations in Nigeria, the North Sea, Colombia and elsewhere; the use of low-cost labour in Asian, Latin American and other countries by the likes of Nike; the development of the 'terminator gene' by Monsanto; the deforestation carried out by logging companies; scientific experimentation on animals. In these instances, the attention of the media is all-important – as is the mobilisation of support through the internet.

The campaigns initiated by activist groups have focused attention on a series of ecological, social and labour issues, and have brought about significant change. Some of that change has been strictly local: Skye residents, for example, won a lower toll rate than that charged to visitors to their island, after a long and colourful protest against the bridge toll operators, ultimately a US bank (which made opposition easier). Many more cases have had much larger consequences: oil companies must now pay far greater attention to the environment in which they work, to local employment and to developing alternative energy sources.

Global movements have been the main drivers of these changes. Governments and global institutions often follow in their wake – elaborating their experiences, expertise and campaigns to provide the basis for codes and legislation. This interrelationship has much further to go, but what must be recognised is that governments in democratic countries remain the only executive force that can claim and mobilise general public support. When governments are returned that do not have an agenda friendly to the movements' concerns, they can claim what the movements cannot: an electoral mandate. The case of the present US administration is the most salient. It is notorious internationally for refusing to participate in the Kyoto Protocol on climate change, while at home it is aggressively promoting both nuclear and coal-fired energy, in spite of safety and waste disposal fears for the former and the effects of the carbon dioxide gases emitted by the latter. Under Bush, the declining coal industry has been

given a renaissance: 22 new plants were proposed between his election and the autumn of 2001. The coal companies insist that they can
make their product 'cleaner', but there is as yet no proven technology
that could make much difference. But new jobs will be created, a
widely perceived energy shortage addressed and powerful lobbies
served. Global movements, faced with such determination, can seek
to step up protest; but frequently they meet resistance not just from
the corporations and the police, but from workers who see their interests in jobs and growth attacked.

The targeting of transnational companies has a further downside,
which is becoming more visible. This is not because they, with government backing, flout the opposition of the global movements;
rather, it can be because they back down and change their behaviour
in the face of activist and media pressure – especially abroad. Many of
the companies targeted for using child labour have now changed
their practices to exclude workers under 18. In some cases, measures
have also been taken to boost family income, but that is probably rare.
More likely, the children – given the poverty of their families – are
still forced to work, but elsewhere, and possibly in worse conditions.
Or take the case of the NGOs' campaign against companies that were
refusing to supply AIDS drugs to African countries at cheap rates.
South Africa, where 20 per cent of the population is HIV-positive,
passed a law allowing the import and use of cheap generic drugs.
Merck and other drug corporations took a case against the South
African government, charging it with violating international trade
rules that governed intellectual property rights – a case backed by the
US government. The case – like that taken by McDonald's against
British protesters – backfired badly, largely because of the opposition
of Médecins sans Frontières, a group that does heroic work in areas,
including war zones, where doctors are generally scarce. The US government backed away, and the corporations announced that they
would sell their drugs at production cost. A clear and moral victory,
but one that loads all costs on to companies that require high returns
to continue lengthy and costly research. The UN's call for a $7bn fund
to combat the disease received pledges of one-tenth of that amount –
revealing that states were happy to let the corporations bear the costs.
Will they continue to do such research? The question is at least worth

asking. The 'solution' of forcing the companies to bear the costs could have an even more unwelcome side effect if it makes the action that African and other states must take to change their citizens' behaviour seem unnecessary. What should be a multilateral contract between governments, corporations, medical services, donor countries and NGOs becomes a morality play with doubtful winners.

Becoming ethical through fear of exposure and loss of sales is unlikely to produce, of itself, good policy. Ethan Kapstein, a professor of economics at the INSEAD business college in Fontainebleau, France, writes: 'Here is where the ethics movement, with its moral certainty, has failed to live up to its potential as a positive movement for change. By focusing attention only on issues that tug at the heart-strings of wealthy consumers, it has left aside those matters that may be even more critical to global economic development, such as the role of multinational firms in technology transfer and human-capital formation. It has dismissed the ultimate importance of governments in shaping a country's regulatory climate, believing instead that it represents some transcendent national or global interest in higher labour and environmental standards. Now that the crusaders have assumed such prominence in the world they must reconsider their responsibilities to those for whom they purport to fight.'[36]

The approach of constructing new networks to address issues of great urgency – such as the AIDS epidemic – is one that some NGOs follow, and from which governments have more to learn. Capitalist business is driven first by profit: indeed, in many states, corporations are obliged to put a duty to shareholders before any other. But the evidence of the past decade is that states and NGOs can work with corporations with success. The UN is encouraging it with a Global Compact; the European Union is working up to a year of global responsibility in 2005; Britain has a minister with responsibility for the issue. The kind of technologies that will be of most use to developing countries – information technologies, new medicines and genetically modified crops with higher yields – all depend on private sector research and development as much as, or more than, that of states, as Mark Malloch Brown of the UN Development Programme has strongly argued. Blanket hostility to the products of corporations can run against the interests of people in developing states.

Genetically modified crops are a striking example. The UN's Human Development Report for 2001 says that they 'offer the hope of crops with higher yields, pest- and drought-resistant properties and superior nutritional characteristics. In China, genetically modified rice offers 15 per cent higher yields without the need for increases in other farm inputs.' Genetically modified crops have been the subject of major campaigns by some global movements, providing another example of where the opposition of activist groups could actually deprive developing countries of a lifeline, and another reminder that few issues can be settled with an easy answer or a simple refusal.

The legal system, which has lagged behind financial and commercial globalisation (except where it is needed for corporate strategy), is now beginning, if slowly, to develop a transnational public law dimension. Corporations face increased challenges from the courts: a growing number of cases are taken against multinationals accused of breaching environmental, human rights, labour and health and safety laws in the countries in which they operate. These cases point to the need for corporations to shoulder increased responsibility for their overseas plants. Indeed, some of the actions are based on a demand that the parent companies provide the same standards as they do in their 'home' countries. These actions are increasingly recognised as lawful. In a case in 2000, around 3,000 South African citizens suffering from asbestosis and mesothelioma won a decision from the British House of Lords – the final appeal court – that they could continue to bring an action against Cape plc, a UK company that had asbestos mining interests. The consequences of these actions are already issuing forth in legislation. The Australian Democrat Senator Vicky Bourne tabled a bill – the Corporate Code of Conduct Bill 2000 – which would impose health, labour and human rights minimum standards on all Australian multinationals employing more than 20 workers abroad. 'A huge range of international agreements is now in place,' writes Halina Ward, a researcher at the Royal Institute of International Affairs, 'that is motivated by a concern to tackle issues of moral concern to mankind. It would be a relatively small step conceptually to join the environmental liability conventions to the body of human rights and labour law by seeking to recognise the justification for international action and internationally co-ordinated liability in cases of egregious transnational corporate abuse of people or environments in developing countries.'[37]

The global institutions: strengthening democratic legitimacy

The global movements' claim that the international financial institutions have not changed in response to their protests is very largely false. These institutions have been in a constant state of change since their creation, and the development of the movements' campaigns has been a major stimulus for further and faster change in the past decade. So much so, indeed, that the major (non-activist) critique of their policies is that they have changed too much for their own – and the developing world's – good because of activists' pressure.

Both the International Monetary Fund and the World Bank – the latter body most closely concerned with development – have, over the 50-plus years of their existence, moved from a relatively simple belief in the virtues of financing infrastructure, through an appreciation of the importance of education and training, to a realisation of and efforts to counter the disastrous effects of macroeconomic instability, to strategies of combining policy advice with financial incentives, to an acceptance that a range of inputs besides capital, including social structures, entrepreneurship and trained labour, were necessary to spur and maintain development. These realisations did not displace each other, but were layered on top of each other in increasingly complex circles of theory and practice. Jessica Einhorn, a former World Bank managing director, argues that 'by describing social goals as inputs rather than results, the bank cleared the path for a cumulative piling on of tasks over the decades, including issues of governance, participation by the poor and anti-corruption'.[38]

The larger problems for the institutions are, in fact, not the immediate ones often raised by the activists – but the coherence of their policies, the realisation of their aims and, above all (this one has been flagged by some activist groups), the strength of their mandate. Even before the activist movement, the Fund, and even more the Bank, were seeking to become more obviously responsive to obvious misery. The appointment of James Wolfensohn as president in the mid-1990s was followed by continued restructuring of Bank priorities, a restructuring that has become even more urgent because of anti-glob-alisation pressure. It clawed away from, without abandoning, a macroeconomic focus, and sought to develop an even broader range of policies to address poverty, corruption, social safety nets, trans-parency, bank reform and corporate governance. At the same time, it opened its doors at least part way to dialogue with the activists – dia-logue that takes many hours of senior officials' time and Bank resources. The result is an overstretch that is now seen as increasing-ly chronic: Einhorn writes that 'the proliferation of knowledge in the last 60 years has led to a complexity of tasks that defies operational definition' and calls for it 'to move both back to basics and into the modern era' – by which she means a radical redefinition or restate-ment of the Bretton Woods aims, coupled with a more modest recog-nition of what it and the other institutions can do to achieve them.

More trenchantly, Stephen Fidler reports[39] that the Comprehensive Development Review launched by Wolfensohn in 1999, designed to 'build stronger participation and partnerships to reduce poverty', is seen by critics inside and out of the Bank as 'a capitulation to the NGOs. Under pressure from NGOs and activists, the bank increasingly has avoided contentious projects such as the construction of large dams. The strategy has helped the institution satisfy its rich-country shareholders and appease critics, though it has not silenced them. Many borrowing [ie, developing country] governments complain it is inappropriate for the World Bank to anoint non-elected, self-styled representatives of civil society to interfere in Bank programmes.' The discontent of developing countries over the welcome given to the NGOs was highlighted in October 2000 in a speech to the Bank's board by the outgoing representative for Argentina, Valeriano Garcia, who criticised 'the strategic thinking of the bank, muddled by too many ad hoc initiatives. We really need to be more focused.'

It is also untrue to claim, as the global movements do, that the IFIs act without consultation with or care for the political and social struc-tures of the countries to which they lend. Indeed, the opposite is often the case: they do not pursue policies that offend these structures, even where the ends are generally perceived as good. Einhorn instances the Bank's approach to the delicate matter of female education in Muslim countries. It backed away from arguing the case that such education should be undertaken as a matter of shared human values or rights. Instead, it argued to the government of Pakistan that higher economic returns would result from female education – a position that allowed it to avoid conflict and outrage, but which had very limited results.

A further example, on which I reported: the Bank's early missions to Russia after the 1991 collapse of the Soviet Union resulted in, among other projects, its identification of the vast and radically underfinanced coal mining sector as one where support would be required to restructure the industry, moving miners out of the often crumbling and uneconomic mines with the aid of grants. But the programme ground into the dust. Post-Soviet politics could not allow the miners, key supporters of the first Russian president, Boris Yeltsin, to be disturbed. The leadership of the mining regions developed a fierce hostility to the Yeltsin government, and saw the World Bank's conditional loans as a threat to the communities perpetrated by the unpopular reformers in his government. Much of the money that was spent disappeared through channels of corruption. Here, as everywhere else, economic change was also social change, and was thus political change. It was stymied because of the political and financial implications to the national, regional or local elites – and these were ultimately outside the institutions' control.

Faced with vast demands, the Bank has long had a tendency to promise too much, given the resources it can ultimately command. The former Ford president turned US defence secretary turned World Bank president Robert MacNamara initiated, in a speech in Nairobi in 1973, a quarter of a century of rhetorical global uplift by committing the world development community to eradicate poverty by the end of the 20th century. The coverage and approval of the world's media for this and subsequent such declarations have proved too tempting for politicians and institutional leaders easily to forgo – especially as they grasp the waste of human life that real poverty always means, and contrast the relative comfort of the rich societies with the state of the developing world. However, for much of the period since the MacNamara speech, the story has been one of sporadic real commitment to extra resources for the poor states. For much of the period, there has been both private and public withdrawal from development, especially in the worst case of all, Africa. The commitments were probably always unattainable by any realistic calculation of development assistance; they became wholly out of whack when contrasted with the reality of a retreating West.

This theme – one stressed by the more experienced activist groups – is a powerful one. The UK government's sharp increase (from a low base) of development assistance is against the trend: the percentage of GDP allocated to development (including the UK's) remains below UN recommended levels. The international institutions have demonstrated, over half a century, a willingness to be flexible, to shift strategy, to respond to criticism, including that of the activists. In the past few years, both these institutions and governments have been active in proposing new financial architectures – including a global financial regulator, a global bankruptcy court and a global central bank. Their problem, and that of the poor societies they would serve, is not their power or their intellectual scope: it is their lack of means.

That the Fund and the Bank have not abolished poverty is obvious, but that they have had, and are having, an effect is as clear. Bank studies of the effects of structural adjustment programmes in the 1980s showed that 42 countries with such programmes had reported 'substantial success' on the macroeconomic front. Russia, which had been a policy battleground within and outside of the institutions because of the high stakes involved in achieving economic reform, has paid the strategy the implicit compliment of its present broad acceptance by almost all strands of political opinion – though huge problems remain on implementation.

The picture of the financial institutions as all-powerful disposers of economic and political power is false. They are more often buffeted by larger powers – especially that of private capital. Very large private lending in the 1970s left many countries – especially in Central and South Americas – with unsustainable levels of debt in the 1980s. These crises, more or less severe, pushed the institutions towards the 'structural adjustment' strategies designed to bring their macroeconomic policies into balance, which crudely offered financial support in exchange for commitments to reduce inflation and budget deficits and to liberalise (including privatise) the economy.

The IMF reforms were aimed to make government 'live within its means', which meant cutting government services and transfer payments, devaluing the currency and boosting exports. The approach did and does cause real hardships: reforms, especially of failing and severely corrupted economies, were bound to do so. The political systems that accepted the IMF plans were at best strained by, at worst could not cope with, the turmoil created by the effects of these moves. Programmes whose basic analysis was formally correct were urged on inexperienced and corrupt governments to be put through at speed, which could not be maintained. Throughout the 1990s, as the West in general and the US in particular grew spectacularly richer (and the rich in these countries most spectacularly of all), large parts of the world, including Africa, the former Soviet Union and many countries in Latin America, suffered falls in income that fell heaviest on the poorest, from which not all have recovered.

The battery of opposition that greets the WTO's activities is based on the belief that the free trade regime it seeks to police and extend is run for the rich at the expense of the poor countries. Furthermore, the extension of free trade into areas such as services, agriculture and cultural products, coupled with the intention of large Western corporations to take advantage of the privatisation of currently public areas such as water, prisons and power in order to extend their reach into developing countries, is seen as the sanctioning of corporate neocolonialism. Friends of the Earth, which has been particularly active against the WTO and the 'world trading system', lists among 'ten reasons why the WTO is bad for people and bad for the planet' charges that it is undemocratic, unaccountable, hostile to environmental and safety standards, erodes cultural diversity, promotes inequality and is open to being 'bought' by large companies.

Friends of the Earth is right that the outcomes the WTO oversees are often harmful to particular groups – often groups of people in poor countries, including subsistence farmers. But in years of campaigning, and in the past few years of targeting world trade specifically, the global groups have not destroyed the argument that the free trading system that has been attempted since the war has been, *grosso modo*, good for the creation of wealth. Nor have they been able to refute the evidence that, the more open that states are, the more likely they are to grow richer more quickly; and that the elimination of trade barriers, though depriving states of revenue, gives customers the benefits of lower prices.

The (many) distortions, inequities and underhand deals done in and around the trading system reflect not the might of the WTO, but the influence of the richest countries and corporations, an influence that can be moderated (and is moderated) only by a rules-based body such as the WTO. Philippe Legrain, a writer who served as an adviser to the WTO director general, argues that 'it is unfortunate that development lobbyists share platforms with protectionists. The main losers from such a perversion of the WTO's mission would be poor countries. For example, to ban [developing countries'] imports because they do not have labour and environmental standards as high as rich countries is to deny them any hope of development – and the ability to afford it in future.'[40] A larger charge against the WTO – one that developed states are not keen to see made – is that it lacks the authority to lever open the markets of these rich countries to the exports of poor ones. Some of the resistance to the WTO expressed by the global movements is, at root, this one: it is one in which both industrial and labour groups can unite on a protectionist platform. Protectionism would be sure to grow if the WTO, or a body serving its functions, were removed.

The responsibility for the left is not to substitute itself for the voice, but to give more of a voice to these poor countries and their peoples. The fault of the global institutions is not so much their own policies, which are often recast to attempt to satisfy the demands of the global movements. It is that they lack a sufficient mandate. In theory, they draw a global mandate from the UN, to which they are subordinate. In fact, the largest influence on them by far is that of the rich states, all of which are directly represented on the governing boards of the Bank and the Fund. Other countries are grouped into (quite large) clusters whose interests are then given to one of the rich but smaller countries' representatives to represent, as well as their own.

This has a kind of justice: the rich countries pay for the operation, and can argue that there should be no taxation without representation. But it does not deal with the larger issues, which the activists have thrown into bolder relief. The perceived slowness and bureaucracy of the international institutions, coupled with the speed and depth of global financial change, has given rise to a growing network of market-based, private international associations, which are now setting standards for global business. This trend throws up the spectacle of a global sphere in which the rules for the corporations are written by their representatives, or at best experts, lawyers and bankers whose businesses themselves depend on the global corporations. Naturally, these laws and codes must be made to conform with national legislation, but in practice the process is often the reverse – that is, national legislation is brought into line with privately developed codes. As Ngaire Woods, a scholar specialising in global institutions, writes: 'the democratic legitimacy of "network governance" relies on a new way of conceiving democracy, which some describe as deliberative democracy; this shifts the focus from the inputs of the decision-making system (ie, elections and representative government) to the quality of the outputs of the system. In this vision, networks of experts provide the opportunity for high-quality deliberation which improves outputs and governance. Scholars are using this framework to justify the inclusion of non-governmental institutions (NGOs) as well as private sector actors in multilateral negotiations. For example, in trade delegations we have seen private sector actors such as American Express taking part under US auspices in negotiations over financial services. The argument is now being used to push for the inclusion in trade negotiations of environmentalists and other transitional NGOs seeking influence on specific issues.'[41]

This approach raises the very large question of mandate and legitimacy. The inclusion of private and NGO actors does not solve the issue; it aggravates it. Neither a bank nor an NGO can claim to represent either 'the consumer' or 'the people': the people must in some form represent themselves. There is currently no better system for such core representation than an electoral one – devalued though it is held to be. It cannot be, especially in a world with so many overlapping layers of interest, the only form of representation, but there seems no democratic alternative to it being the central one.

This recognition does not exclude, but must make use of, the development of network-based and deliberative approaches to complement the core representation of states and citizens. Indeed, using networks to link activists and the like-minded has been one of the successes of the centre-left in the past few years, as policy forums to discuss ideas of progressive governance have blossomed in both the political and academic arenas. Network organisations can be a source of renewal for fading associations such as political parties as much as a threat of their replacement. But we cannot escape from the central insight that legitimacy is gained, albeit indirectly, from citizens in represented countries giving their consent.

Thus the governing boards of the institutions must be widened to include representatives of the developing nations. It is impossible to get change that is firmly 'owned' by developing states when the structure of the development bodies excludes them as mature actors. The institutions, and the states, are thus forced to work in a system that resembles the franchise in 19th-century Britain: one where there was representation, but based on the notion that only property could confer the requisite responsibility of judgement, and thus deserve the vote. The masses were excluded because they were deemed prone to usher in communism through the ballot box. The history of the 20th century, however, was much richer in examples of masses who laid the basis for communism, or other authoritarian systems, because they were deprived of recourse to the ballot box.

The assumptions about liberal economies, free trade and macroeconomic stability are not the issue here: they have been shown to benefit many countries, and their reverse – full (North Korea) or partial (Cuba) autarchy – has certainly been shown to consign states to continuing poverty and authoritarianism. These assumptions, however, will certainly change in detail, and may well change in substance. But they cannot be properly adopted by the political and social cultures of states if they continue to be imposed. The antidote is thus more strength to the institutions of democratic government nationally, and more representation of governments in the governing structures of the Bank, IMF and other global agencies. It will be more cumbersome; there will be high costs in delay. But there seems to be no other route to acceptance of reform.

We need more politicians: policies for a global political agenda

How to avert the steady worsening of Henry Kissinger's view of the world rent into a rich and sophisticated minority and a poor and disabled underclass? How to put flesh on the bones of Tony Blair's vaulting rhetoric? How, that is, to bring about real change in a world in which the system that delivered, and still delivers, great wealth to the rich societies is seen by many in the developing world – often rightly – as offering nothing, or less than nothing, to them?

One of the minor, and still unfolding, lessons that 11 September taught the West was a moratorium on the use of the word 'crusade'. It became starkly obvious that, for those who see themselves as oppressed, history is not chronological but flat, with the key events arranged as on a collage – where the medieval invasions of Muslim lands can be placed in the same frame as the creation of the state of Israel or the Nato victory over Iraq. In fact, 'crusade' should have been quietly dropped long ago: for it has been misused in verbal commitments – against poverty, against division, against disease – too often to retain a meaning. What is required is not a new crusade: it is the measured and sustained creation of the means and institutions through which a world, now conscious of itself as a unity in a way it has never been before, can address its direst problems. It is the challenge of making politics global.

David Held, the British political scientist who is a leader in developing thought on the issue of global governance, puts the problem both starkly and clearly: 'If the most powerful geopolitical and economic forces are not to settle many pressing matters simply in terms of their own objectives and by virtue of their own power, then the current institutions and mechanisms of accountability need to be reconsidered.'[42] The global movements have correctly pointed to the numerous instances where the most powerful forces do settle matters in the service of their own objectives, and because they have the power to do so. These movements' very existence is testimony to the fact that this approach causes resentment and opposition to these powers to grow, and to become more entrenched and violent.

The policy lines that the centre-left now has the responsibility to develop, and to convert into generally accepted strategies, draw on many of its sources of inspiration. The largest shift is to make these concretely, rather than merely rhetorically, global.

First, the centre-left has no choice but to accept and proclaim the consequences of its radical revisionism. It needs the capitalist system to work; it has no theory or practice for its replacement or supercession; the state, on which it had relied to achieve a slow march towards socialism, is currently not capable of the task, even if a coherent socialism were available. The logic of that position is to develop part-nerships with capital as well as with the groups of civil society to assist in the achievement of its aims.

New Labour would seem to need few lessons in that respect. But with it goes another logic. That is, that the representation of the pop-ulation within a country cannot be effected, at the core, by other than an elected government. The devaluing of politics and politicians, whether effected by the global movements, by the media, by corpora-tions or by the politicians themselves, has been and remains a move-ment replete with danger for our societies. As much or more than ever, they remain the indispensable medium through which conflict-ing pressures and interests can be resolved. Politics does not require to be surpassed: it must be reasserted and renewed. Only politicians with a mandate can occupy the state and use it as a means to bring pressure to bear on other actors in what it perceives to be the com-mon good. Competing versions of what the common good means is still the defining ground for the clash of party and interest.

Social democracy has been absorbed in a project of capturing the centre. It must use that position as a base from which to widen and deepen the acceptance of social responsibility and liberal practice. It can no longer do it nationally: national protection against global trends and pressures is not negligible, but has limits with which we have become familiar. Governments are constrained to act trans-nationally. They must do so from a national base: an increasingly complex operation.

Tony Blair's speech to the Labour Party conference in autumn 2001 was remarkable not just for its high idealism, but for the fact that it operated on a global, not a national, canvas. Few leading politicians used a major speech to the most active sections of their parties in that way in the 1990s – the decade, after all, of the most rapid globalisa-tion. It was called forth, of course, by the events of 11 September, and it marked a sudden shift back to the concerns of British politicians up to the 1950s, when Britain finally ceased to have any claims on the first rank of global power, and when politics became largely domestic.

Politics has again become global, for an indefinite time in the future. It is a further (possible) good that may come out of evil. It forces politicians and electorates to address what has previously been the preserve of diplomats, NGOs, multinational corporations and banks and the global movements. In becoming global, in a world in which uncertainty and danger are higher than they have been for decades, politics must again become central, finding new springs of support and idealism where before these were atrophying.

Second, the search for global institutions and mechanisms is now an urgent one. In a paper for the Open Democracy internet journal[43], David Held and Mary Kaldor identify three major areas in which the construction of these institutions must begin: a commitment to the rule of law, not war; the creation of a new form of political legitimacy, and a recognition that the ethical and social justice issues posed by the global polarisation of wealth cannot be left to the markets to resolve. Commenting on these priorities, they write that the alternative to an 'old' reflex of a largely military response is 'to recognise the novelty of the contemporary situation, to learn the lessons of earlier "new wars" and the profound difficulties of achieving a meaningful military victory, to involve people in a political and not a military process, and to ensure that political ends and means mesh in the pursuit of justice'.

Some of the possible mechanisms have already been mooted here. They include the broadening of the mandate of the international institutions – not merely to take in and attempt to satisfy the demands of the global movements, but to give the developing countries a larger stake in the process. This will not be a formula for improving the efficiency of the institutions' strategies; it will have to cope with their own need to keep their credit ratings high in order to borrow. But they need to hear a stronger and more constant voice from the poor and poorest in the world – and to amplify that voice to governments (who control the IFIs) and the lenders. The global financial institutions have become central to the legitimacy of the system: where it is seen as losing legitimacy as it increasingly is, their actions cannot simply be ad hoc and palliative. It comes back to politics, to finding the electoral support from within the cultures of contentment that have been Western societies for a conscious and sustained engagement with a much rougher and poorer world whose contours we only vaguely see.

For the European Union, the challenge is a different one. Its slow and conscious construction as a centre that will take over some of the functions of its member states has produced a unique hybrid, somewhere between an international organisation and a nation state. It is well suited to the modern world in one sense: its necessity to mediate and compromise between differing levels of authority gives it the ability to work with states and groups outside of its borders with greater flexibility and less implied threat. However, its lack of a central voice and authority can also cramp it: its response to the 11 September attacks was, if immediately supportive, slow in substantive response. The issue of military assistance was immediately regarded as a national one – especially, but not only, by the UK. If it is to continue with what many of its initiatives promise – an extension of the reach and influence of a zone of peace and law – it will need to develop a willingness on the part of its member states to allow a central executive to frame and decide on issues that are currently held tightly in the control of the major member countries.

Third, the 'factor of production' that is less mobile than others in the age of globalisation – humanity – must now be treated as fully human: a constant and central concern of the left. Among the issues that have been treated as national but are now increasingly global are: the migration of the poor to the rich states; the selection by the latter of the educated elites of the former to bolster public and private services; the provision of education to countries where its availability is severely limited, and the creation of work, especially for the young, in countries where there is little of it. If these exercises are not to be merely means by which the developed world protects itself from the poverty of the developing countries, the plans developed must be put to governments and electorates in all states affected as areas of mutual engagement and responsibility. The ideas and examples generated in the UK by the Treasury and the Department for International Development on debt reduction and to combat poverty have been among the most constructive.

In the past two decades, states, international institutions and NGOs have developed experience and practice in conflict resolution and prevention, a sphere that has drawn the major countries increasingly into armed interventions in internal conflicts in the Balkans, Africa and elsewhere, such as East Timor and Haiti. Many in the global movements see these, in a more or less undifferentiated fashion, as imperialist adventures. The lesson drawn by centre-left governments is the opposite: it is where governments have withheld intervention, such as in Rwanda, where the largest horrors have been perpetrated. It is one of the reasons behind a historic shift in military posture, foreshadowed by a speech in the German parliament in late October 2001 by Gerhard Schroeder, the German Chancellor, in which he pledged German forces for 'participation in military operations to defend freedom and human rights and to create stability and security'. However, these humanitarian interventions lack rules, and there has been little debate (outside of polemics) about their scope, limits and effectiveness. If they are to play a major part in military thinking and preparation in the rich states, the left must make this a larger issue.

International criminal law, which has the aim of bringing developed as well as developing states under its aegis, has been among the most heartening of developments in the past decade. It has a long history: its modern manifestations can be traced to the efforts, from the mid-19th century, to give rules to the conduct of war (legality of weaponry, treatment of prisoners and civilians) while remaining agnostic on the legality of war itself, and on the culpability of its progenitors. After 1945, which saw the trials of German and Japanese officials on war crimes charges, a concept of 'crimes against humanity', and thus of criminals against humanity, entered into political and legal discourse. Until our own times, the conventions of humanitarian law have lacked a police force and a judicial centre: as Lawrence Wechsler puts it[44], 'although the various conventions and codes project a magisterial all-inclusiveness, what they've most pointedly lacked, at least until recently, has been any effective means of enforcing the magisterial norms, and specifically of holding individuals criminally accountable both to their victims and the world community, for their violation'.

The present stage of development seeks to put these on a firm footing. The establishment of the ad hoc criminal tribunals on Rwanda and Yugoslavia and the surprising moves to establish the International Criminal Court in the latter part of the 1990s have given the movement towards an international criminal law a huge boost – even if it is one from which some of the rich states, most obviously the US, now recoil. Yet the implications of the observation of Justice

Richard Goldstone, the first prosecutor at the Yugoslavia war crimes tribunal in The Hague, are not easy to evade: 'Inter-ethnic violence usually gets stoked by specific individuals intent on immediate or material advantage, who then call forth the legacies of earlier and previously unaddressed grievances. It is they, not the group as a whole, who need to be held to account, so that people will be able to see how it is specific individuals in their communities who are continually endeavouring to manipulate them.'

Fourth, the left has to recognise and overcome the very strong resistance to political globalisation, which is at the same time its imperative. The project of global governance, or cosmopolitan democracy, is likely to be seen by many states, at least by their ruling groups, as a threat, rather than as an opportunity. A commitment to spread social justice to women as well as men will be repelled by most Islamic societies. A demand that all be free to speak, write and vote as they wish will not be accepted in China. The notion that globalisation is, in developing and/or authoritarian states, a kind of subversive movement to which the more open, intelligent and enlightened members of these societies join is beguiling – it underlies much of Friedman's *The Lexus and the Olive Tree* – but it is remote from a certain kind of reality. It is true of some among an urban intelligentsia – though it was precisely members of that class who committed the terrorist acts on 11 September, committing suicide in doing so. It is not, and cannot be, true of the poor, who are in the very large majority.

Talking to states and cultures, which wish to keep themselves as far as possible inviolable, about common rules is hard. If there is to be a concept of global justice, it must be one that draws from other traditions than the Western. Yet these are often based on wholly different assumptions, codes and traditions: for all sides to be satisfied with an agreed conclusion will require huge compromises. But the alternative route – to insist on purely western standards, or to pretend that there is general assent to formally approved codes on human and civil rights that are seen as Western in inspiration – is the present situation, and it is clearly failing.

This is the area where most thought must be given and work done. At one extreme – explored by the political philosopher John Gray in *Enlightenment's Wake*[45] – there is nothing more that universalist visions and codes can do, because there is a 'global counter-movement against Westernisation underway in many parts of the world, in which Occidental ideologies are repudiated and Western ways of life spurned'. Gray believes that non-Western cultures accept technological advance while scorning most or all of its culture: he proposes, as a slim chance of 'finding a path through the ruins in whose shadows we presently live', the 'willingness to share the earth with radically different cultures ... not [as] a means of promoting ultimate convergence into sameness, but rather an expression of openness to cultural difference'. A different, though not opposite, opinion is held by the economist Amartya Sen,[47] who quotes the Bengali poet Rabindranath Tagore as saying 'Let me feel with unalloyed gladness that all the great glories of man are mine' and continues with a scornful dismissal of the view that some cultures do not value or aspire to 'Western' freedoms – 'the case for basic freedoms and for the associated formulations in terms of rights rests on 1) their intrinsic importance, 2) their consequential role in providing political incentives for economic security and 3) their constructive role in the genesis of values and priorities. The case is no different in Asia than anywhere else, and the dismissal of this claim on the grounds of the special nature of Asian values does not survive critical scrutiny.' Sen also believes that Western approaches to development are 'too respectful of authority', and calls for a stimulation of popular participation in development. Between or within these approaches, ways must be found to construct that which can get broad recognition as a neutral and equally welcome space for a discussion of justice and respect. To dismiss this as a mere exercise in cultural relativism, or in dilution of core values, is to misunderstand the challenge now facing the world.

Social democracy renews itself through challenges. It has many in its domestic heartlands, but it can no longer confine itself to these, for they will not be answered by domestic responses. In seeking to become global and transcending the boundaries of national state politics, however, it takes upon itself a task that has only previously been attempted through empire – but without recourse to empire's coercion. How that is to be achieved, with what institutions and through which forums, is the task for social democracy now: 11 September makes it harshly clear it cannot be delayed.

Notes

1. By global movements I mean the organisations which have appeared, for the most part in the last decade, which actively oppose 'capitalist globalisation'. Included in their critique are most or all of the global institutions which act as forums for the powerful states (Group of 7/8; European Union; Organisation for Economic Co-operation and Development), regulate trade (World Trade Organisation), supply capital (International Monetary Fund) and assist development (World Bank). These movements are distinguished from the usually older groups which exist to fight poverty and assist development, and which I refer to as non-governmental organisations, in the customary way. There is, of course, a fluid boundary between these, and a number of groups – such as Greenpeace and Friends of the Earth – move constantly to and fro across them.

2. Lapham, L. (1998) *Waiting for the Barbarians*, Verso, London

3. Newsweek International, 30 July 2001

4. Financial Times, 10/11 February 2001

5. Fukuyama, F. (1992) *The End of History and the Last Man*, Hamish Hamilton, London

6. Ohmae, K. (2001) *The Borderless World: Power and Strategy in the Interlinked Economy*, Harper Collins, New York

7. Kissinger, H. (2001) *Does America Need a Foreign Policy?* Simon and Schuster, New York

8. Samuel Huntingdon (1996) *The Clash of Civilisations and the Remaking of World Order*; Simon and Schuster, New York

9. Reynolds, D. (2000) *One World Divisible*, Penguin, London

10. UN Economic and Social Council Report, 1994.

11. Castells, M (2000) *End of the Millennium: The Information Age, Economy, Society & Culture vol. III*, Blackwell, Oxford, p.203

12. The Guardian, 12 October 2001

13. see Giddens, A. (1994) *Beyond Left and Right*, Polity Press, Cambridge; Giddens, A. & Pierson, C. (1998) *Conversations with Anthony Giddens*, Stanford University Press, Stanford; Beck, U. (1999) *What is Globalization?* Polity Press, Cambridge

14. Beck, U. (2000) *Post National Society and its Enemies*, Prometheus/04

15. Wolf, M.J. (2000) *The Entertainment Economy*, Penguin, London

16. Gray, J. (1998) *False Dawn: the delusions of global capitalism*, Granta Books, London

17. Stokes, J. & Reading, A. (eds.) (1999) *The Media in Britain*, Palgrave, London

18. Savio, R. private memorandum, July 2001

19. George, S. & Saabelli, F. (1994) *Faith and Credit*, Penguin, London

20. Luttwak, E. (1999) *Turbo Capitalism*, Texere Publishing, New York

21. Klein, N. (2000) *No Logo*, Flamingo, London

22. Bunting, M. (2001) *From socialism to Starbucks*, Renewal, Spring 2001

23. Hertz, N. (2001) *The Silent Takeover*, Heinemann, London

24. Frank. T. (2000) *One Market Under God*, Secker & Warburg, New York

25. The Guardian, 17 August 2001

26. The Guardian, 15 August 2001

27. Financial Times, 11 September 2001

28. New Left Review, July/August 2001

29. Financial Times, 11 September 2001

30. Limes 3-2001, 'I Popoli di Seattle'

31. Le Monde, 11 August 2001

32. Friedman, T. (1999) *The Lexus and the Olive Tree*, Harper Collins, New York
33. Sen, A. (1999) *Development as Freedom*, Oxford University Press, Oxford
34. Cooper, R. (2001) Foreign policy, values and globalisation. In: *Global Ethics:* Demos Collection 16, Demos, London
35. Economist survey, 'The New Geopolitics', 31 July 1999
36. Foreign Affairs, September/October 2001
37. 'Governing Multinationals'; RIIA briefing paper, February 2001
38. Foreign Affairs, September/October 2001
39. Foreign Policy, September/October 2001
40. Prospect, May 2000.
41. Renewal, February/March 2001
42. Giddens, A. (ed.) (2001) *The Global Third Way Debate*, Polity Press, Cambridge
43. Held, D. & Kaldor, M. 'New war, new justice?' www.OpenDemocracy.net, 28 September 2001.
44. Gutman, R. & Rieff, D. (1999) *Crimes of War*, WW Norton, New York
45. Gray, J (1995) *Enlightenment's Wake*, Routledge, London
46. Sen, A. op.cit.